AF552664

"So long as we love, we serve, So long as we are loved by others
I would almost say that we are indispensable and no man is useless while he has a friend."

R. L. Stevenson

Written in one of Ebenezer Teichelmann's Christmas Cards to friends

The Life of Ebenezer Teichelmann

Ebenezer Teichelmann

Pioneer New Zealand mountaineer, explorer, surgeon, photographer and conservationist

Cutting Across Continents

Bob McKerrow

Foreword by Sir Edmund Hillary

tara-india research press, new delhi

tara-india research press
B-4/22, Safdarjung Enclave,
New Delhi – 110 029.
Ph.: 24694610; Fax : 24618637
bahrisons@vsnl.com
contact@indiaresearchpress.com
www.indiaresearchpress.com

ISBN : 81-87943-87-4

Cataloguing in Publication Data
Ebenezer Teichelmann
Pioneer New Zealand mountaineer, explorer, surgeon, photographer and conservationist
Cutting Across Continents
Bob McKerrow

Includes bibliographical references and index.

1. Mourtaineering 2. Biography 3. Exploration 4. Conservation 5. Doctor
I. Title II. Author.

Printed in India at Focus Impressions, New Delhi – 110 003.

Foreword

As a young climber I came to respect the climbs and exploration done by Dr. Ebenezer Teichelmann, mainly from the West Coast of New Zealand, up those long and difficult valleys such as the Cook River Valley, and his many first ascent were remarkable in that day and age of hobnail boots and long handled ice axes. His third ascent of Aoraki Mt. Cook in 1905 was a wonderful achievement.

I have seen his photographs gracing many NZ Alpine Journals and other books and I am delighted that hardy band of West Coast mountaineers which included not only Dr. Teichelmann, but Peter and Alec Graham and later, my old climbing partner, Harry Ayres, is getting the recognition they deserve.

Both Dr. Teichelmann and I are former Presidents of the NZ Alpine Club and I am pleased the club is supporting this important publication on New Zealand Mountaineering, and capturing a bygone era of courage and tenacity in exploration.

Sir Edmund Hillary
1 December, 2003.

Contents

Foreword	Sir Edmund Hillary	vii
Introduction	Bob McKerrow	1

His Life

Chapter One	Beginnings	9
Chapter Two	The man	15
Chapter Three	The Doctor – war and peace	31
Chapter Four	Social Involvement	59
Chapter Five	Conservation	77
Chapter Six	Mentors: G.J. Roberts and Charlie Douglas	91
Chapter Seven	Through the Lens	103
Chapter Eight	From goldmining to mountaineering	115

The Expeditions

Chapter Nine	- 1900: Exploring the Fox Glacier and Victoria Range	123
Chapter Ten	- 1902: First Crossing of Graham and Baker Saddles	127
Chapter Eleven	- 1903: Up the Fox Glacier to Pioneer Pass	137
Chapter Twelve	- 1904: First Crossing of Pioneer Pass	141
Chapter Thirteen	- 1905: Harper Saddle and Mount Cook	149
Chapter Fourteen	- 1906: Cook River and Mount La Perouse	159
Chapter Fifteen	- 1907: First ascents galore – Head of the Fox Glacier	171

Chapter Sixteen	- 1908: The toughest yet – Waiatoto	183
Chapter Seventeen	- 1909: Climbs from the Tasman Glacier	193
Chapter Eighteen	- 1910: Rakaia and Whitcombe Pass	199
Chapter Nineteen	- 1911: Unraveling mysteries of the Lambert & Lord	203
Chapter Twenty	- 1912: From the Footstool to Switzerland	211
Chapter Twenty-one	- 1914: First Ascent of Mount Spencer-three dead	219
Chapter Twenty- two	- 1924: Perth River and Sealey Pass	225
Chapter Twenty-three	- Retirement	231
Chapter Twenty-four	- 1934: Newton returns	241

Acknowledgements and photo credits 249
List of Ascents and explorations 255
Glossary of mountaineering terms 258
Glossary of New Zealand words/terms 259
Index 261

Publisher's Note

Having worked with Bob on this book, you cannot imagine how he feels for *Ebenezer Teichelmann.* He has literally lived *Ebenezer's* life during his research. There may not be much that he has left out from his study.

This most authoritative work by Bob McKerrow is an in-depth biography of *Ebenezer Teichelmann:* the man, the surgeon, the mountaineer.

Anuj Bahri Malhotra

Introduction

Mountains have dominated my life since I was 17. In 1966 while climbing up to Ball Pass under the shadow of Aoraki Mt. Cook, I heard the name of Ebenezer Teichelmann for the first time from a grizzled old climber. As the years ticked by I found I was coincidentally walking in his footsteps. The more I read about this exceptional man, I slowly discovered he had a relationship with the mountains unlike any other I had read or met. Different from Herman Buhl, Eric Shipton, Edmund Hillary, Gaston Rebuffat, Walter Bonatti, Rob Hall, Reinhold Messner, Alison Hargreaves, Lydia Bradey, and their ilk.

Teichelmann worked at the feet of mountains curing people who were sick or dying and if requested, he operated on their beasts of burden, the people's work horses.

Friend of ferrymen, gold-miners, publicans, prostitutes, farmers, explorers, speculators, rock-solid working women, fishermen, sailors, shepherds, saw-millers, tunnelers, blacksmiths and shop-keepers who lived on the edge of life, at the end of the world.

Teichelmann lived on the periphery of the mountains and he felt their pulse and moods in his daily work, travels and life. The watery arteries of the snow, ice and mountains often blocked his passage as he tried to reach patients needing urgent medical treatment. He fell in love with their shape, light and curves and sensitively captured their moods on his large plate camera. There was a sense of intimacy in his photographs and writing, and when he was moved by the beauty around him, would often quote from Longfellow, Stevenson or other romantic poets. He was in love with Mary, a beautiful and unconventional women.

The rains she knew in Scotland and England were not unlike the rains of New Zealand's West Coast, which sometimes fell incessantly for weeks, formed by westerly air currents forming over the wild Tasman Sea, and dumping their moisture as they rose up and hit the western side of the Southern Alps.

Toiling seven days a week for a year on end as surgeon, gynecologist, anesthetist and general practitioner where life and death paraded in its many guises, his annual expeditions became a balm for his burnt out body and brain. His scientific bent and a surgeon's eye for detail, helped him understand the nuances of cartography, and he built on the work of early surveyors and explorers, filling in a few final blanks on the map.

Searching for final snippets of information about Ebenezer Teichelmann finished for me, 91 years to the day after he stayed in the English Alpine Club rooms in the Gornergrat Hotel, situated at 3130 metres on the Gornergrat Ridge, close by to the Matterhorn in Switzerland. He was 53 when he sat on the same terrace when I started writing this introduction on 23 August 2003. Books have to finish sometime and I couldn't think of a better place.

After looking at the passes he crossed, the glaciers he walked and the two peaks he climbed here, I felt a sense of completion watching the view in front of me which seemed so symbolic of his expansive life.

The peace and tranquility he felt in 1912 in the Swiss Alps was to be shattered less than two years later when the country of birth of his mother declared war on the country of the birth of his father, and he joined the New Zealand Expeditionary Forces to fight on the side of the British.

Strangely, I finished the first draft way back on 6 November 1993 before leaving for three years to work for the Red Cross in Afghanistan. Like good wine maturing, the book slowly mulled as more of his photographs came to light, experts challenged and contributed to my draft, and more information was unearthed.

It was with a great deal of excitement I returned to New Zealand in 2003 as my friend Colin Monteath had an album belonging to the Canterbury Mountaineering Club, which had been lost for 30 years or more, and recently rediscovered in a garage in Christchurch. The joy I felt opening the album containing 600 of his 5 by 4 inch contact prints was overwhelming and enabled me to display his superb photographs freely in this book.

By 2003 I had now either seen or climbed all the peaks and passes he had crossed, the scenic reserves and national parks he advocated for, and visited nearly all the cities in England, Ireland, Germany, Austria, Australia, Egypt, France, Greece and New Zealand he had worked in as a Doctor or surgeon.

The West Coast of New Zealand was my home for nearly ten years: two years I lived at Franz Josef Glacier and seven years in Hokitika, where Ebenezer Teichelmann spent over half of his 79 years. There in the early 1990s I was able to interview people who knew very him well. Many are no more. Their stories always had a touch of admiration, humanity, detail of deeds done, and often humour. What stood out was that he cared for people, and those close to him were not afraid to use the word 'love' to describe one of Teichelmann's strong emotions, for example, "He had that rare gift of always seeing the very best in his friends, for he especially loved and had much consideration for young people, and I always felt he loved us in spite of our faults; yet withal; he was so amazingly modest about his own gifts and especially concerning mountaineering achievements," said Peter Graham. In annual Christmas cards he sent to friends he picked out quotes that immortalized love and friendship, and illustrated with his most beautiful photograph. He was a caring and sensitive man. But he still remained a source of curiosity. Few, if any, truly understood this man of a character so different to theirs.

I cycled and walked many times from his former house in Hokitika up to Westland Hospital where he was Medical Superintendent for almost thirty years, often stopping at the cemetery where he and Mary lie side by side, or stopped at his clinic close to the Red Lion pub where he enjoyed a drink, the Carnegie Free Public Library that was a dream, and the houses of friends he visited, and the harbour he left by ship for medical and exploration journeys. On clear winter days, I could look at most of New Zealand's highest mountains and passes in the distance, many climbed for the first time by Teichelmann.

Many of his climbs and journeys I repeated, some of them up almost impenetrable valleys, such as the Callery, Burton, Spencer and Cook.

During periods of intensive research and travels in his footsteps, I got incredibly close to what it would have been like to be him.

At times I struggled to find what made this remarkable man tick, but the more I talked to people who knew him, I slowly brought together his many faces; doctor, surgeon, public health promoter, mountaineer, explorer, photographer, conservationist, world traveler, philanthropist, philosopher, humanitarian, gardener, soldier, promoter of free-public libraries and tourism, tennis player, swimming, golf and cricket club president, newspaper director, Trustee Savings Bank pioneer, admirer of abattoirs, harbour board chairman, and a rationalist by faith. A canvas as wide as the world.

Born in the Victorian era he saw photography develop, the birth of the telephone, the motor car and the aeroplane and unbelievable advances in science and medicine.

Interviewed regularly, he wrote little for such an eminent man but thankfully, a record of his mountaineering and conservation efforts survive on negatives, prints and publications scattered throughout New Zealand and are of a stupendous quality.

This book is not a strictly chronological account of his life - until you get to the expedition chapters half way through the book - as I believe by trudging the reader through a chronological sequence it would rob the reader of the extraordinary impact he achieved in the various facets of his life.

Ebenezer Teichelmann drank life to the lees. It was hard to find someone to say a bad word about him except when he took on conservation battles or when his German sounding name was criticized by racists.

On Kornergrat Ridge, outside the hotel where he stayed in 1912, I lifted a glass and drank to Ebenezer Teichelmann. It was a rich red wine from the Swiss Valleé.

Bob McKerrow

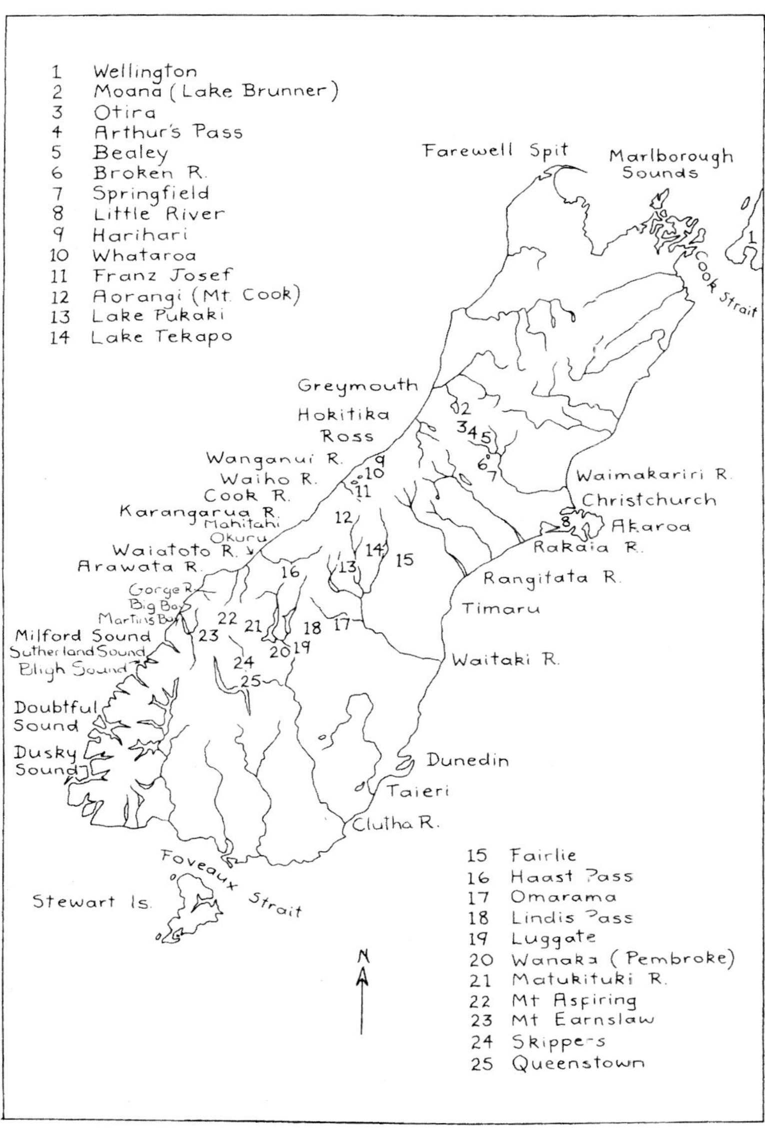

South Island New Zealand

His Life

Beginnings

There was a loud CRACK above. Eyes swiftly swiveled up to witness a huge block f crumbling rock slowly tumble and disintegrate, then plummet, sweeping all before it. he sun had been warming the slopes for most of the day. The tenuous grip of spider-ebs of ice was loosened enough, and with nowhere to hide, a volley of humming rocks scaded down. With a clatter of ricochet and the smell of Hades they flew past. Silence turned. No-one had been hit. This time.

The ridge was like a knife. Any thoughts of jumping over the opposite side to hold partner's fall would be suicide. The parting of hemp fibres would not even be noticed in e swift descent.

Above soared a rock face, dropping like a forehead from the summit brow. Creases ice knitted together large expanses of bare rock. Here the climbing was technical and emanding. Flashing axes occasionally sent out showers of tinkling frozen crystals as elicate steps were cut for boot edges. Numb fingers caressed the rock for any projections at might offer relief from the drag of gravity. Skillfully weaving a vertical path, the two imbers stalled at the base of a smooth, featureless slab. The summit appeared to be only rope length away, and time was racing by. Tom removed his alpine boots and slipped on ibber-soled friction shoes for the rock. Even so, he could gain no height. Some combined ctics were necessary: a push from Malcolm Ross. Tom Fyfe slowly disappeared from ew.

Malcolm was uneasy. The rope had been moving with a nervous manner. Now it opped.

'Have you found a good belay, Tom?' queried Malcolm.

'Not really,' he replied.

This meant that the protection offered by the rope above would be solel psychological. Any slip by Malcolm would be fatal to both climbers.

Totally focused on the climbing, Malcolm carefully eased his way higher. Som tentative assistance with a tight rope was needed to start, but he concentrated on th delicate shifts of balance, and the play of rhythm and opposing forces. Quickly To resumed the lead, abandoning his axe for freedom of movement.

Soon they both stood where no-one had been before. This was the North Peak c Mount Haidinger, 3061 metres high in the Southern Alps of New Zealand, and the da was 1897.

The long ascent had taken many hours, and they still had to descend before darkne fell. Tom went first, confidently down climbing the difficult sections, but always awa that Malcolm was just above. Should he slip, both would plummet down the steep cliffs the ice far below. As quickly as they dared, they made their way to the rope-eater ridg Tom retrieving his ice axe at the base of the slab. But luck was running out.

Malcolm led now, down a particularly rotten section of rock. Despite his best effort Tom could not avoid dislodging some rock onto his partner below. Unable to evade th bombardment, several struck Malcolm: a solid thump to the leg almost knocking him o the mountain, and then another blow to the shoulder. But this was no place to linge Only minutes later disaster was narrowly avoided when another large flat one glanced hi on his helmetless head. Had it been the sharp end, he may not have survived with just struggle for consciousness.

There were still some serious sections to negotiate, but eventually they reache snow slopes that could be safely slid. Unroped on the final rocks, they hurried downwar This was a section of schist, lying in sheets and slabs, poised to strike. Some had vicious sharp edges. Malcolm's axe turned crimson when one sliced his hand. Tom lost a piece his leg after one nasty blow to the shin. They could only treat themselves as best possible with their meagre resources, and plod homeward.

Mount Haidinger

They crawled into the safety of their bivouac at de la Bêche, on the edge of the 'asman Glacier, on nightfall. Forrest Ross, Malcolm's wife, was there with William Iodgkins. The extent of the injuries was soon thrust aside with the pleasure of eating. 'he planning of further adventures in animated conversation after the evening meal kept ıeir minds on more pleasant pursuits.

Malcolm recovered from his head injury to continue climbing with Tom, ascending Iount de la Bêche in four hours forty, then on to the Minarets. No complaints from Tom bout his leg were recorded, but the injury worsened during their epic exploration over .endenfeld Saddle and down the Whymper Glacier. Despite finding a hot spring for a elieving bathe, Tom had difficulties getting to sleep due to the pain of his injuries.

Whymper Glacier

Matters did not improve the next day. Travel is awkward in the rugged and almo impenetrable Whataroa Valley, and he further damaged the leg negotiating the first gorg The bad leg was knocked on sharp angular rocks twice in succession. Infection was ragin he had a feverish temperature, and the leg had swollen to a ridiculous size. The pain di not diminish. Sleep was fitful and fleeting.

Nearing the end of their pioneering trip, Tom was swept off his feet and tumble towards the final gorge. Driven to survive, he scrambled out just in time, but the pain c his leg was now so great that he admitted later that it would have been a relief to drow

After several days of rest and farm remedies in Rohutu, it was no better. The on option now was to continue up the coast to Hokitika for medical treatment.[1]

1. Malcolm Ross. *A Climber In New Zealand.* 1st Ed. Edward Amold. London 1914

About the time Malcolm Ross and Tom Fyfe were organizing supplies and equipment for their climbs of Mounts Haidinger, de la Bêche and the twin summits of the Minarets, a train was hissing to a stop further north in Hokitika. Amid the bustle and steam of a busy station emerged a curious figure. So slight was his stature that it could be mistaken for that of a thirteen-year-old boy. Thin wiry legs stood askance, rooted firmly to the ground in wide-welted leather boots. His attire had a European styling unusual to the district: tight stockings to knee-height with woolen knickerbocker pants. A sports coat of similar weave clad the lightly-framed torso. He wore a hat on a head of coarse dark hair, and beneath its brim sparkled lovely grey eyes that spoke of intensity and compassion. Delicate, finely-boned fingers clasped a pipe that he replaced between a fine set of teeth. A whiskery goatee beard jutted forward, reminding one of a Captain Cuttle figure.

Hokitika - 1870

Beside him stood his pretty wife, Mary, beneath a broad-brimmed hat with flowing feathers. Her dress was more typical of the period, with a long dark skirt, tight bodice, and a small jacket. The quality revealed cosmopolitan origins; a step above what was sold around the corner in Tancred Street draperies and milliners. A subtle smell of expensive perfume was discernable.

Hurrying to meet them was the head of the Hospital Board, for this new arrival was the recently appointed Medical Superintendent of Westland Hospital, Doctor Ebenezer Teichelmann, and his wife Mary.

On 27 February 1897, just a few days after the Doctor set up his practice; the injured mountaineer Tom Fyfe limped into the surgery of Dr Teichelmann for an examination of his leg. Several pieces of bone were removed, and a course of treatment for necrosis of the tibia was prescribed. This meeting was to change the course of the Doctor's life. His curiosity was aroused as to what lay south of him in the misty mountains and what motivated men to explore them.

The Man

As Ebenezer and Mary walked down the gravel footpaths of Revell Street in Hokitika for the first time, they must have been struck by the rawness of the town, in stark contrast to the more familiar streets of London, Dublin, Birmingham, Paris, Edinburgh and Adelaide. Hokitika still had visible remnants from its rough gold mining heritage. Many of the town's businesses were still trading in buildings erected hastily in 1865 to sell goods and services to the thousands of miners in the surrounding districts. The narrow and winding Revell Street had four imposing banks located handy to the river in the old business area, ready to buy the now diminishing return of gold. The sections along Revell, Tancred and Sewell Streets were narrow tent-site-sized postcards of land. The beach, at the back of the Revell Street shops, was an unpleasant sight, with household and commercial rubbish strewn about, including offal and decaying animal products dumped by the numerous slaughter houses found backing onto the waterfront.[2] When the wind blew from the westerly quarter, the stench was overpowering.

The uneven graveled streets were laid out in a grid pattern, and away from the town they meandered through remnants of forest. Small wooden cottages, with verandas, tin chimneys, and corrugated iron roofs sent plumes of smoke across the town from wood burning stoves and open fires. Canvas dwellings were evidence of the transitory nature of many of the inhabitants. The wide open drains running alongside the streets carried water, either from the old creek beds which once snaked across the town, or storm water during the heavy rains. These drains were a constant source of danger. Many pedestrians

---

2. Ron Fields, *Place of Return - Hokitika Borough Council 1869-1989*. West Coast Historical Museum, 1989. p80.

fell into them when wending homewards after dark. They also carried life-threatening diseases, and were a source of tragedy as young children were often swept away into the river during floods. Behind the bustling wharves along Gibson Quay swirled the brown waters of the Hokitika River, swollen with recent rain. The fresh south-westerly wind was cleansing the air of the last of the clouds, revealing the serrated edge of the Main Divide.

Once famous in the late 1860s as the busiest ports in New Zealand, if not the world for a brief period of time, with tall ships bringing thousands of miners from the Australian gold fields, and importers shipping in a huge tonnage of goods to meet the needs of the surrounding gold fields, the river port was now almost deserted. Deforestation of the river flats for farming had contributed to the silting up of the river, and the bar now claimed several shipwrecks.

Hokitika Wharf 1868

This port had seen some of the South Pacific's most colourful and deviant characters such as Bully Hayes, the blackbirder and pirate who arrived in his brig Rona in late 1866 from the Fiji Islands with the following cargo-50,000 oranges, 50,000 limes, 1000 cockatoos,

80 pigs, 200 pineapples, 200 citrons and a quantity of South Sea Curiosities, which on inspection by the customs officer, found "a number of young native Belles."[3]

The odd trader still left the river heading south to take goods to settlers at Okarito, Bruce Bay and Jackson Bay.

Not far from the wharves were the presses of Hokitika's two newspapers: in newly built premises in Revell Street was the Hokitika Guardian, with its Liberal political stance; and the West Coast Times, which also held liberal views but directed constant sniping and ridicule at the politics of Premier Richard John Seddon. From January 1897, the Princess Theatre was delighting patrons with an entertaining night out at the new sensation known as cinematograph. Average nightly takings were reported at around one hundred pounds. The position of Medical Superintendent (sometimes referred to as Surgeon Superintendent) was advertised for a suitably qualified person to serve the area from the Taramakau River to the north to Jackson's Bay in the south, stretching over 380 kilometres of the roughest terrain in New Zealand; subject to floods, avalanches, mud-slides, wind storms, earthquakes and storm surges from the sea.

Dr Ebenezer Teichelmann was 38 years of age when he arrived in Hokitika on 11 February 1897 with his wife, Mary, to take up that position at the Westland Hospital. Competition for the position had been fierce: the selection committee received forty-seven applicants and spent three evenings narrowing the selection down to four names. The results of the first ballot show a tie: Teichelmann 7, Grieg 7, Cribb 2, Brown 2. Another ballot was held with Dr Teichelmann receiving six votes and Dr Grieg three. Dr Teichelmann's credentials would have been impressive, and his experience gained in England, Ireland and Australia gave him the advantage.

Ebenezer's father, Christian Gottlöb Teichelmann was born in Dahme, a small town about 60 kilometres south of Berlin, Germany in 1807. He was the second son of Friedrich August Teichelmann and his wife Johanna Rosina. By trade Friedrick was the 'clothmaker of Dahme.'[4]

---

3. NZAJ 1992. Winter Ascent of Red Lion Peak by West Coast Publican. P11, Bob McKerrow.
4. Wm. Bruce Kennedy. *Lutheran Missionary to the Aborigines-Pastor Gotlöb Teichelmann. 1807-1888. His Family. Life & Times.* (Privately published by he author 1989. Coolangatta. Queensland)

Christian Gottlöb Teichelmann

After spending ten years at school, Christian Teichelmann was apprenticed as a carpenter for four years, a trade he liked. Once he became a journeyman he worked in a number of towns in Saxony and Prussia, before moving to Berlin. While working as a carpenter, he took private tuition and qualified in 1830 for entry to the Building Institute School in Potsdam. While there, he met pupils of the Jaenicke Missionary Institute and at the age of 25, entered Jänicke's Missionary Seminary, and completed his training at the Dresden Lutheran Missionary Society Institute, and was ordained in 1838 at Altenberg. He emigrated to Australia that year traveling from Hamburg to London, and then set sail on 21st May 1838 to South Australia as a Lutheran Missionary to work among Aboriginal people in South Australia. He accompanied Clamor Wilhelm Schürmann. The passage was very quick as the ship was carrying the second Governor of South Australia, Lieutenant-Colonel George Gawler and arrived in Australia on October 14th at Holdfast Bay.

Shortly after arrival, they immediately set out to learn and document the Kaurna language.

Christian Teichelmann was a gifted linguist arriving in a new country speaking not only German his native tongue, but French, Latin, Greek and Hebrew learnt during his six years of training, and English and very quickly he gained fluency in the aboriginal

ABORIGINES OF SOUTH AUSTRALIA.

ILLUSTRATIVE AND EXPLANATORY

NOTES

OF

THE MANNERS, CUSTOMS, HABITS, AND SUPERSTITIONS

OF THE

NATIVES OF SOUTH AUSTRALIA.

BY

C. G. ~~R. T.~~ TIECHELMANN,

GERMAN MISSIONARY TO THE ABORIGINES.

Adelaide:

Published for the benefit of the German Mission to the Aborigines, by the Committee of the South Australian Wesleyan Methodist Auxilliary Missionary Society.

1841.

Cover of Christian Teichelmann's First Book

language of the Kaurna people to the extent where he could instruct them and establish an open air school for their children on the banks of Karrawirraparri (the Torrens River) at a place still known as 'Pinky's Flat'. A proper school was opened in December 1839 not far away from the first site on the north side of The Torrens, opposite the site of the present rail bridge, then known to the Kaurna people as 'Piltawodli.[5]

Missionary work in the field is very different from tra-ining in a seminary and Teichelmann and Schürmann struggled enormously but they stuck at it and remarkably after only eighteen months in the country published a description of the language, entitled *Outlines of a grammar, vocabulary, and phraseo-logy, of the aboriginal language of South Australia, spoken by the natives in and for some distance around Adelaide.*[6]

"Two years we have been living amongst this people, and we have left nothing untried, as far as our means admitted, to civilize and influence them by the Christian truth, at least with those with whom we came in frequent contact. First we endeavoured to acquire their language to a certain degree, which lasted more than a year, before we came so far as to converse with them upon more serious subjects, as their language was but imperfectly known," he wrote in his booklet, 'Aborigines of South Australia.'

Christian Teichelmann fought against the strong racism shown by many Australians of European origin and got close to his Aboriginal friends through working with them, helping them build houses, digging and planting in their fields. In his publication he vigorously opposed allegations that they were a lower form of life and wrote "they have the same abilities, talents and intellect as us." It was some of their habits and customs he disapproved. In 1840 they were joined by Pastors S Klose and H. Meyer.[7]

Teichelmann's gift for languages was recognised by the Governor of South Australia and he was appointed in May 1840 as "Interpreter for the Aborigines" and he gave up his teaching in the school.

---

5. Ibid. p8.
6. Dr. Rob Amery. *The First Lutheran Missionaries in South Australia and their contribution to Kaurna language reclamation and the reconciliation movement.* CESGL. University of Adelaide. Sept. 200 pp 30-35.
7. Bill Edwards. *The First Outback Mision. The Moravian Mission at Lake Kopperamanna.* University of South Australia. undated.

The numbers of children at the school had dwindled from a peak of 50 to less than 12. The Governor, well-meaning citizens and the missionaries began to see the destructive effect on the Kaurna people by concentrating them on the fringes of European settlement.

In a move to get to a more remote area, Christian Teichelmann purchased on November 1842, section 502, Hundred of Noarlunga, which he named Ebenezer Settlement. It is interesting to note that a dream of a life time, setting up his own mission station, he named Ebenezer, the name he would give to his son who carried his own dreams, not those of a Christian missionary, but those of a famous surgeon, and a rationalist by faith. Ebenezer settlement was in the Happy Valley of the Wimmera District and was also known as Happy Valley. Here Teichelmann rolled his sleeves up and built a simple mission station and working with the local Kaurna people, started cultivating the land and teaching them settled agricultural practices. By now he was reasonably fluent in the Kaurna language when suddenly in early 1843, Governor Grey made a rule that English would be the language taught as it was deemed useful progress could not be made by teaching in localized dialects. This order, coupled with the nomadic spirit of the Kaurna people who would go walk about when the urge came, spelt disaster for this new mission.[8]

Missionaries like Teichlemann had virtually no more than the clothes they stood up in and their Bible. This meant they were not able to attract or bribe their attention by gifts of food, trinkets or money but had to meet the aborigines of their own terms, man to man. "They had to grow vegetables themselves, or spend from their own poverty stricken pockets."[9]

Ebenezer's mother, Margaret Nicholson, was born in Edinburgh, Scotland, where she lived with her parents until they all sailed in 1840 to Australia. She was fifteen years of age. Her father, Daniel Nicholson, set up a business as a wine and spirit merchant. While at Happy Valley at the age of eighteen, she married Christian, then aged 36, on 25 December 1843, in the Presbyterian Kirk, Adelaide. Marrying in a Scottish church, outside of the strict Lutheran congregations, started a rift between himself and the Lutheran congregation in the years to come.

---

8. Wim. Bruce Kennedy. p.10 op. cit.
9. Ibid.

They lived in a mission house on the banks of the Torrens River soon after their marriage. After Margaret and Christian married, they had fifteen children: seven boys and eight girls. Ebenezer was number nine in this large family. The children were named Frederick, Daniel, Jessie, Christian, Johanna Rosina, Charlotta, Johanna, Margaret, Ebenezer, Maria, Emmanuel, Theodore, James, Alfred and Josephine. Ebenezer was born on March 23, 1859, near Callington, South Australia.

Christian Gottlöb Teichelmann struggled to bring up his family on the pittance received as a missionary, and returned to Adelaide in 1846 and by late 1847 'had ceased to occupy the Government supplied mission house on the bank of the Torrens and was living, in straightened circumstances, on a small farm at Morphett Vale.' He continued to minister to some of the congregation in Adelaide, while supporting his growing family by his farming activity.'[10]

By returning to Morphett Vale the family life style went from bad to worse for the Pastor, Margaret, Fred not yet three, baby Dan and newly born Jessie. The 80 acres of land they settled on was poor farming land.

Margaret had many difficult years with her father dying in August 1843, four months before her marriage, and her Mother died in April 1846. She had just turned 20. Her Father died without a will so the whole estate went to her brother in England and she didn't get a penny. Five more children were born in Morphett Vale and only three lived past infancy. Johanna Rosina died in 1853 from scarlet fever at 8 months of age, and Alfred died the same month as a premature baby. His birth was recorded but not his death.

Fellow missionary Pastor Schürmann writes in letters dated 1852 of the poverty and difficulties the Teichelmanns suffered, "these fellows are badly off and " too poor to move".

The family eventually moved to Salem a district about four miles from Callington and then later to Red Creek farm in 1860. Five more children were born here.

---

10. J.F. O' Donnell. *The Descendants of Christian Gottlieb Teichelmann. Lutheran Missionary to the Aborigines in the Colony of South Australia.* 1974 and C.G. Teichelmann. *Aborigines of South Australia. illustrative and explanatory notes of the maners, customs. habits, and superstitions of the natives of South Australia.* 1841.

It was at Red Creek farm that Ebenezer or young Eb as he was called, moved as a baby, just a few months old. Not much is recorded about his early years but it is clear the Teichelmanns were a tight-knit and deeply religious family, with hard work and the Bible being the cornerstones of their Lutheran-led, and Presbyterian influenced, life.

One hundred and sixty years after Christian Teichelmann wrote his classic publication *Outlines of a grammar, vocabulary, and phraseology, of the aboriginal language of South Australia, spoken by the natives in and for some distance around Adelaide*, a paper written in 2000 by Dr. Rob Amery an expert in linguistics at the University of Adelaide, on the First Lutheran Missionaries in South Australia, pays tribute to the exceptional work done by Teichelmann and Schürmann to the Kaurna Aboriginal language reclamation and reconciliation process. Had they not made the dictionary at the time, the language which was lost, could never have been recovered.[11]

Young Ebenezer was a very studious young man and along with his brothers, worked on the family farm. Medical records show he was kicked by a horse at a young age, leaving him with scars on his right leg. From early childhood, Ebenezer Teichelmann was filled with dreams of becoming a doctor or a surgeon. He boarded at Handorf from 1869 until 1873 and out of all the family, he was the only one who did not move to the Yorke Peninsula in late 1873 or early 1874. Ebenezer had ambition and didn't want to be a struggling farmer all his life and managed to get apprenticed to a Chemist in north Adelaide. After completing his apprenticeship he moved to Port Adelaide as a dispensing chemist to a doctor while continuing his medical studies matriculating at Adelaide University.[12]

He traveled to England in 1882 to study medicine at Queens University in Belfast and Mason's Colleges in Birmingham. Specializing in surgery, Ebenezer Teichelmann did post graduate studies at St Bartholomew's Hospital in London, and later at Dublin Hospital in Ireland. Once qualified, he acted as Demonstrator of Physiology at Mason's Science College in Birmingham.

In Birmingham, he took up a position as Resident Medical Officer for the Birmingham Workhouse - a place for paupers and derelicts, enacted in the sixteenth century

11. Dr. Ron Amery. op cit., ps 30-58.
12. Wm, Bruce Kennedy, op.cit. p 53,

under the English 'Poor Laws'. Here he gained valuable experience in the realities of life, and the consequences that political decisions have on the physical and mental health of those trampled under the economic scrum. Ebenezer Teichelmann was brought up speaking English and German,[13] and it is likely that frequent contact with Aboriginal people in Australia through his father's mission work instilled compassion from an early age for the less advantaged. He certainly did not have the arrogance and intolerance of others that seems to blight some well-educated westerners.

Mary Teichelmann

Later positions included Assistant Physician and Resident Pathologist at Birmingham General Hospital, Assistant Surgeon at Jaffray Suburban Hospital, Resident Medical Officer at Birmingham Workhouse, and private assistant to Mr. Lawson Tait (a well known gynecologist) in Birmingham. He also had a private practice for two years in England.

Dr Teichelmann's father died in 1883, while Ebenezer was training in England. Thirteen years later while working in Hokitika he received word from Australia that his mother, Margaret Teichelmann, had died on 30 March 1906 at the age of eighty-two.

While in Birmingham, he met and later married Mary Bettney, a former matron of a Birmingham hospital.[14] In 1886, his older sister Charlotte gave birth to a boy, and named him Ebenezer Thomas Kendall.[15] In 1890 he married Mary.

13. J.F. O'Donnell, op. cit.
14. Graham Collection, Teichelmann file, Hokitika.
15. Kendall Genealogy, Australia :website: members.fortunecity.com

In 1892, Dr Teichelmann returned from England to Melbourne, Australia on board the Anchor liner Yarrawonga as the ship's Doctor. Behind his name were the titles, F.R.C.S. Fellow of the Royal College of Surgeons, M.R.C.S (Eng) Member of Royal College of Surgeons, Eng-land and L.R.C.S. (Ireland) and Associate of Mason's College (Birmingham). Fifteen years earlier he had been an apprentice to a chemist and now returned a highly qualified surgeon. On arrival he moved to Port Adelaide where he filled the post of Health Officer.

An undated newspaper clipping, which is likely to be 1892, records his return to Adelaide.

> Dr. Teichelmann returned to this colony by the steamer Adelaide from Melbourne on Thursday after an absence of nearly ten years, during which he has been engaged in the study and practice of medicine and surgery in the City of Birmingham. Dr. Teichelmann was educated in this colony, and before leaving for England, was assistant with the late Dr. Gething and Dr. Toll at Port Adelaide.[16]

For almost five years from May 1892 until his Hokitika appointment in February 1897, he served first as a Surgeon Lieutenant, then as Surgeon Captain in the South Australian Military Forces. By now he was married, and a surgeon and physician of considerable experience. By 1895 he and his wife Mary, had a registered lease of rooms on North Terrace where he was practicing as a surgeon. In the same year he was appointed locum tenens for Prof. E.C. Stirling, Physiology Professor at Adelaide University, who was visiting England. At this time there was a dispute between the Adelaide hospital and its medical staff, and Dr, Teichelmann was offered the post of Senior Surgeon with the right of private practice. To quote his own words many years later "... as I did not care to go back on any brother professionals, I refused the offer. My one chance in Adelaide was gone and I decided to go away."

He and Mary looked for a change and Teichelmann applied for and gained the position of Surgeon Superintendent in the Westland County Hospital based in Hokitika, New Zealand a position that required him not only to be an experienced surgeon, but a

---

16. Graham Collection. Hokitika - Teichelmann files.

good administrator and to provide medical services to people scattered over 380 kilometres of the remotest coastline in the world.

Hokitika was quite a sight to the Teichelmanns when their train chuffed down the narrow strip of coast from Greymouth. The land looked intimidating, with large tracts of lowland forest, and patches of rough pasture wrested from the bush by pioneering farmers and miners. On the right swept the Tasman Sea, arching waves with feathered spray, spawned in southern ocean storms. But directly ahead, looming above the buildings of Hokitika, stood the regal massifs of Mounts Cook, Tasman and Elie de Beaumont.

Lake Mapourika, South Westland

Ebenezer soon established himself in the local community. This was relatively easy for a Doctor, as people were generally appreciative of the skills and knowledge that he had to share with them. Despite the demands of his employment, Ebenezer sought out other involvements. Mary Teichelmann became an active participant in the local community, and an avid supporter of the Westland Hospital. In 1897 she received a vote of thanks for collecting the sum of eight pounds, eight shillings and four pence to procure an invalid chair.[17] But behind the façade of being the Doctor's wife and doing expected duties, she was a strong individual who lived life to the full, without too much regard for social expectations. She was an emancipated women and was the first woman in Hokitika to smoke publicly, using an elegant black cigarette holder, and was one of the first women to play golf and drive a motor car.[18] She threw conventions aside, as did Ebenezer her husband, but in the rough and ready ex-gold town, they got away with it. They were slightly different, but that did not prevent them earning the respect of others. "Tender", "loving" and "respectful" are words others used to describe their close relationship.[19]

Hokitika was quite a cosmopolitan community, comprised of a wide range of nationalities and personalities. While different in some ways, the Teichelmanns were definitely not eccentric outsiders.

The egalitarian society was one he believed in. Maori and European he viewed with similar respect. The barriers of race didn't exist for Teichelmann. Often when queried about his own heritage of a German father and Scottish mother he would say, "I have a Scots body and a German brain."[20]

The Doctor's reference to having a German brain may have been said in jest, but Teichelmann did have some characteristics which could have only been inherited from his German father, and those characteristics highlight the difference in attitude between the British and German/Austrian outlook on life.

In addition, Austrian and German visitors to New Zealand had modes of

17. West Coast Historical Museum: Teichelmann files.
18. Hec Davidson and Dorothy Fletcher, personal conversations. 1993.
19. Ces Preston. Hec and Elsie Davidson, information pieced together from their parents and relatives, personal conversation. 1992.
20. Elsie Davidson, personal conversation, June 1993.

communication that were different from those manifested by Britishers. The former were more gregarious in social relations, more philosophical in reflection, less solemn about the trappings of British authority and less judgmental about Maori life and behaviour.[21]

Mary Teichelmann

The year 1909 started off well for Ebenezer Teichelmann and on his return from the Mt Cook region he shared his elation with Mary and showed her the photographs of one of his most enjoyable expeditions with Dr Vollman and three West Coast guides, Alec and Peter Graham and Darby Thomson. Speaking German for more than a week was a joy and then, as always, he sent a guide to dispatch a telegram to Mary, informing her he was well and safe. His closeness to Mary is easy for someone of this generation to

21. Michael King, *The Collector*, Hodder and Stoughton, 1981 pp 29-30.

feel and interpret, but in that era when she was Mrs. Doctor Teichelmann, and in the background, the intimacy of relationships was not discussed openly. Her disdain for convention and submission was noticed and admired by some. Playing golf, being the first woman to drive a car in Hokitika and smoking in public, saw her as a trend-setter while at the same time, putting her aside from others.

Twelve years in New Zealand had slipped by quickly for Mary and Ebenezer. They were a popular couple, warm at heart, community minded, elegant in appearance, sophisticated in knowledge and showed grace, charm, wit and according to oral history handed down from parents of those who knew them well, they appeared to be a couple deeply in love.[22]

Like a thunderbolt from nowhere on Thursday 20 May 1909. Mary, at 46 years of age, died suddenly of a heart attack. Ebenezer Teichelmann was devastated. Two days later she was buried in the Hokitika cemetery.[23] The West Coast Times records her death:

> "Quite a gloom was cast over Hokitika yesterday afternoon when it became known that Mrs. Doctor Teichelmann had died suddenly. For the last four days the late Mrs. Teichelmann had been indisposed, and late in the afternoon yesterday she was taken seriously ill. Doctor MacAndrew was immediately summoned and on his arrival pronounced life to be extinct. Unfortunately Doctor Teichelmann was absent at Blue Spur, and although word was sent to him of his wife's illness, the end came before he reached town. Sincere regret will be felt in all parts of Westland at the sad and unexpected occurrence.[24]

What feelings must have run through his mind when driving at break-neck speed along poorly formed dirt tracks across the hillocks in a new car from Blue Spur just having been informed that Mary was seriously ill in Hokitika? Somehow, he usually made it to the bedside of so many people who were seriously ill, or dying, but the torment of probably not being not there for own wife when she really needed him.

---

22. Jim Keman. Ces Preston, Hazel Kelley, Hec and Elsie Davidson. Nell Stevenson. Kelly Wilson & Jack Banister, Personal conversations, 1992.
23. Graham Collection. Death sighting, Mary Teichelmann
24. West Coast Times.

On arriving in Hokitika his dear friend Dr MacAndrew broke the news that Mary had died of a heart attack. Ebe was devastated. She was the centre of his world, his stability, his confidant.

Together they had met in England, traveled extensively in England and Scotland, sailed to Australia where they lived for five years, and then traveled by ship to New Zealand.

> "So long as we love, we serve
> So long as we are loved by others I would
> almost say that we are indispensable
> and no man is useless hile he
> hase a friend."

On a Cristmas card later that year, his favourite lines from Robert Louis Stevenson appeared.

MacAndrew and Teichelmann with Scottish genes and blood running through their veins, were joined in mourning by fellow explorers, surveyors and Scots; Duncan Mcfarlane, G.J. Roberts and Charlie Douglas. Surely William Bannister would have joined, said his grandson when his group of friends gathered.[25] Did they have a few drinks together to drown their sorrows and try and console their dear friend? Scots and Scotch mix easily in times of sorrow.

On a green hill, overlooking Hokitika, Mary Teichelmann was laid to rest on Saturday 22 May 1909.

---

25. Jack Bannister, personal conversation, Nov. 1992.

The Doctor—war and peace

Seaview Hill is a magnificent viewpoint on a terrace above Hokitika. The coastline sweeps north to Punakaiki and the Paparoa Range, and curves south to Mounts Cook and Tasman and the sub glacial forests. Spreading around in an alpine amphitheatre to the east is the Main Divide, and the many lower peaks that range down the river valley. On this site Westland Hospital was built in 1877.

The hospital was a place you would stay for life if you had bad luck or the wrong chemistry, you could be born, receive medical treatment, operated upon, jailed, put out to graze if you were too old, incarcerated in a lunatic asylum and buried in the cemetery nearby. A one-stop. At the time of Dr. Teichelmann's appointment of 11 February 1997, it contained four wards capable of holding a total of fifty patients. But it was a bizarre, almost macabre, collection of facilities. Westland Hospital provided maternity, surgical, medical and geriatric services. The Seaview Lunatic Asylum was added in 1872, and at the time of Teichelmann's arrival, it had 120 patients, of whom 35 were women. Near was the local jail, with an average occupancy of 12 prisoners. It had 20 cells for men and 10 for women. For those who no longer needed any solace of this earthly realm, the cemetery, also on Seaview Hill, provided space for eighty-four burials in 1897.

Just south of Seaview Hill on the flats between the hill and the river lies the main residential areas of Hokitika. Close to the sea is the commercial centre. In the midst of all this is Cass Square. In a tradition continued to this day with the Hokitika Wildfoods Festival, a large picnic was held there in mid-February. The long grass was cut in Cass Square to make room for the 1,500 holiday makers arriving by special train from Brunnerton

Unloading from ship at Bruce Bay - 1920

and the Grey Valley. The air warmed under the glow of an amiable sky and western hospitality.

But four days later the lifeless body of a newly born baby was found in the Stafford Street drain. 'It certainly doesn't look like a Hokitika baby!' claimed the West Coast Times. As one of his first public duties, Dr Teichelmann gave evidence at the inquest, and after constant rumour and counter-rumour, which went on for weeks, a woman from Dobson was eventually discovered to have been the child's mother.

Dr Teichelmann could initially be consulted by his private patients at his rooms in Kellers Hotel, known now as Stumpers, on the site of the former Westland Hotel. In May he hired a builder to construct a residence on the site of the old Sir Henry Barkley Hotel in Hampden Street. Within three months he was advertising that patients could be consulted at his new residence opposite the old fire station in Hamilton Street, next to the Carnegie

Taking supplies along Gillespie's Beach - 1931

building. The building survives to this day and acknowledging its former owner, it is now called Teichelmann's Central Bed and Breakfast.

The Doctor's area of responsibility was from the Taramakau River to the north down to Jackson's Bay past Haast. South Westland was a wild, untamed area that attracted pioneering and adventurous souls.

Beautiful and remote, the landscape was also unforgiving and harsh. Numerous trips for medical and surgical calls were required, and the severe, undeveloped nature of the travel was such that these trips hardened Dr Teichelmann for future climbing expeditions. Long time friend, W. A. Kennedy, describes the conditions the Doctor had to travel in:

Roads in those early days were few, and transport bad. Below Ross, little more than pack tracks existed and the rivers were unbridged. Under such circumstances dogged determination, coupled with judgment, was often necessary to get safely through. This quality the Doctor fortunately for all concerned, possessed in a marked degree, a quality which later served him in good stead during his exploring and alpine adventures.[26]

Dr. Teichelmann (Centre) preparing to go down a mine at Ross

Accidents were numerous as men broke in new land, mined for gold or toppled tall trees. This 'frontier' existence often meant was often called upon to respond to disasters. Being in good physical shape, Dr Teichelmann was always willing to go to the scene of accidents, often with scant regard for his own life.

Towards the end of 1897, eight buildings were destroyed by fire in the south end of Revell Street, just around the corner from the Doctor's surgery. It started in the old wooden Golden Age Hotel, which had stood on the same site since the gold rush days of 1865. Next door the Hokitika Guardian office was soon ablaze, its contents completely destroyed. The fire took with it a large slice of West Coast history, for the newspaper files since 1865 were destroyed, along with those of the Evening Star. People rushed out on the street as dense plumes of smoke and savage licks of flame erupted from the stricken buildings. The capricious wind was a continual handicap but eventually the fire was brought under control. The next day only a few gaunt chimneys and masses of twisted corrugated iron marked the spot where the business houses stood. The shop owners stood amid ruins of their livelihood, thinking that December 1897 day the blackest of their careers. Fortunately no one died, but a number of people were treated by Dr Teichelmann for burns and smoke inhalation.

26. *The Canterbury Mountaineer. 1939. p98.* W.A. Kennedy: 'In Memoriam, Dr. E. Teichelmann 1859-1938:

The following year, on 7 September 1898, a terrible mining tragedy occurred at a goldmine at Craig's Freehold, across the river in South Hokitika. When word reached Hokitika that a fall of sand and earth had buried some hapless miners, the Doctor left immediately, crossing the river by boat, and going to the mine to ascertain for himself the nature of the accident and what probabilities there were of the entombed men being recovered alive.[27] Unfortunately three men died that day. But accidents did not only happen during business hours.

One night the moon had not yet risen over the alps, and the darkness pressed down from above like a coffin lid. A few stars managed to peer between the high clouds at their reflection in the swirling river. Fifty metres away the sounds of a staggering, clanking drunk reeled across the water. A fog of faint light from curtain-filtered windows wafted upwards. Into the night, high above the black water, shrieked steel wheels on rails. Two figures, barely visible against the dark horizon, urgently pushed and pulled the handles of the jigger. They had over ten kilometres to go to reach a sick patient at Ruatapu. On one end sat the thin, wiry figure of Doctor Teichelmann, urging on the protesting vehicle. Assisting him was his dedicated nurse, Bess Hudson.

Dr Teichelmann, without a care for established conventions, had employed her at a time when the occupation was mostly dominated by male nurses. The decision to employ Bess arose partially due to the Doctor extending his private medical practice to include a nursing home to accommo-date short-term patients. Bess, his first nurse, was a daughter of John Hudson, Hokitika's first storekeeper. The Hudsons did not approve her choice of career, but she put herself into the work with enthusiasm. Her uniform was a white and lilac striped uniform with starched white apron, cuffs, collar and a cap. For her services, she received five shillings a week from Dr Teichelmann, and felt quite wealthy. Bess loved her work.

Teichelmann was a hard but fair employer. Bess was on call from six in the morning to midnight. She recalled many years later. "He never asked me to go out—he just ordered me to. I was always there, whenever I was wanted."[28]

---

27. West Coast Historical Museum, and Anne hutchison of Hokitika assisted with the research for this chapter, and most of the unlisted sources have come from the hokitika Guardian/West Coast Times files.
28. West Coat Times Special Supplement, Mrs B. Winter: 'Nurse Bess Hudson', May 1, 1992.

The Hokitika railway bridge, 1900

Teichelmann was a busy man with his medical and surgical work keeping him fully occupied. He still managed to find time for his conservation work, his many committee meetings, and all the other philanthropic and charitable work that demanded his attention. A casual flick the the West Coast Times for 1907, reveals some of the events involving the Doctor that came to the attention of the local paper:

On 8 January he attended a man injured in a horse and cart accident at Kaniere bridge. A week later he left for his annual climbing trip to South Westland for four or five weeks. Dr Macandrew was his locum during his time away. On 20 March he gave evidence at the inquest of Yhu Chung, a Chinese mental patient who had died at Seaview Hospital. April 4 was the Westland Hospital Trustee meeting. Dr Teichelmann gave a summary to them on the sanitary conditions at the hospital. The next day he attended to Mrs. M. J. Hall, who had been dead in her home for at least twenty-four hours. She had been the former licensee of the Golden Age Hotel. On 23 April there was an accident at the Arahura dairy factory to attend. In May, he gave evidence to the inquest for Robert Sweeney, who was found dead in the street from hypothermia; and Annie Brown, seventeen, who died as a result of injuries received by an explosion of benzene. In October there was a failed suicide attempt at the Michel Brothers' farm at Kowhitirangi. A young man tried to kill himself by taking carbolic acid and then shooting himself with a pea rifle.

On 17 October the Doctor made a record trip to Okarito. He received an urgent call at 2:00pm on Tuesday and left Hokitika at 3:00pm, arriving in Okarito at 12:30am the next morning. After attending to the patient, he left at 8:00am the same day, and arrived back in Hokitika by 7:15pm. He had covered 174 miles, mainly on horseback, and in a little over twenty hours.

Sometimes it took 1-2 weeks to reach remote communities such as the Nolan Homestead at Okuru.

On 20 December, the Doctor was summoned to an unusual incident. This time he hurried around the corner from his surgery to the Café de Paris in Tancred Street. Upon his arrival, he was ushered over to a table in a darker corner. A man was seated there, unaccompanied. It must have been a quiet time of day, as his head was face down in a bowl of water, and on the back of his head, to hold it down, was a clothes trunk. John Scopinich, aged sixty-seven years, had drowned himself in a public restaurant, using a bowl of water.

Dr Teichelmann's visits to the Arahura area, just north of Hokitika, were frequent. He would make house calls to patients up the valley, and later at the Arahura Pa.[29]

While at Arahura, he always stopped at the dairy factory where a number of families lived. The manager was John Cameron, a man of Scottish parentage and originally from Otago. An event in 1911 must have stirred memories of his wife's death, some two years earlier. Elsie Cameron, the factory manager's wife, was expecting her first child. She was 23 years and had only been married eleven months. It was an event that she and her husband John had looked forward to, but complications arose during pregnancy. Dr Teichelmann diagnosed her condition as eclampsia, which was often fatal in those days when drugs and antenatal care was minimal. It is a condition which brings on epileptic convulsions caused by anatomical lesions.[30]

The Doctor delivered a baby girl on 28 June 1911. John Cameron named her Elsie after her mother. Elsie Cameron (now Davidson) said later, 'My mother never saw me. She just took fits and convulsions for the four days she lived after my birth. It was quite a complicated affair.'[31]

Dr Teichelmann must have been devastated at seeing a young mother die four days after giving birth, leaving a young baby. Although there was no fault on his part, he obviously felt a heavy responsibility. 'That's why he became attached to me I think, and I was a bit of a favourite to him. Dr Teichelmann always seemed to take a special interest in me. He would always come into the dairy factory, pick me up, and take me on his rounds of Arahura. He had a big coupé,' recalled Elsie Davidson.[32]

Operations are a private and often a gory thing and surgeons rarely write about them. There are frequent but very general references to the many operations he performed on kitchen tables, benches and makeshift operating tables, but not the technical detail. Recently, Jonathan Kaplan, a South African surgeon who served as a hospital and battlefield surgeon, wrote about the excitement and tragedy of being a surgeon and it gives an insight to the high and lows of this highly skilled art..

29. Elsie Davidson, personal conversation, June 1993.
30. Ibid.
31. Ibid.
32. Ibid.

There is a unique thrill to operating. Opening a belly, for example, and knowing how the layers of the abdominal wall will cleave under the line of the knife. The skin, bronzed by sterilizing iodine, must be opened in a single sweep, for its elastic tension pulls the wound ends apart, and later extension to the cut will look dog-eared and ragged. Under the skin lies fat; creamy or a rich yellow, dense or semi liquid, according to body type and diet. As it parts. the first drops of red are starting from the cut surfaces. They are promptly sealed by cautery forceps, and a wisp of blue smoke and a brief smell of barbecue rise under the theatre lights.

Then comes the muscle layer, easiest to split along its fibrous junction in the midline. This must be divided with care, for immediately beneath it lie delicate structures: the sliding contents of the abdominal cavity and the delicate film of the peritoneum that sheaths them. The cut gapes like a buttonhole. You slide your fingers in the muscle sheath-the first intimate contact with the patient-and the steel jaws advance, clipping through fibres that grit faintly between the steel jaws.[33]

Kaplan goes on to describe the thrill of operating but also the horrific side when opening the abdomen:

The first thing that will strike you is the smell, the reek of an abattoir. A swill of blood, bile and faeces obscures the clean structures, signifying ruptured vescera and torn vessels. Bowel can wait a while for patching; bleeding can't, and while the anaesthetist pumps transfusions into neck and arm veins, the surgeon looks for where it leaks, and he sweats. Even old hands, veteran operators, feel the fear as dark blood rises from down where the great vessels lie. Sometimes I still dream about the feeling of helplessness when my knowledge seems useless against the implacable approach of death.[34]

For a surgeon operating in one of the remotest corners of the globe, Teichelmann pushed himself beyond his own self-imposed limitations, and in moments of self-doubt, may well have wished he had fellow surgeons to turn to consult.

Devastated by the death of Elsie Cameron, soon after came another death which must have haunted him. It was the death of Hugh Graham Preston the owner of Preston's

33. Jonarthan Kaplan. *The Dressing Station*, Picador. 2001, p17.
34. Ibid. p 18

Bakery. 'My father died of peritonitis and there was no cure for it in those days,' said Ces Preston.[35]

It must have been a searching time for Dr Teichelmann. He is likely to have asked himself if there was anything more he could have done to save Hugh Preston and Elsie Cameron. These two deaths and many others led Teichelmann to go overseas to learn the latest developments in medical treatment. The West Coast was becoming too isolated. In fact he felt New Zealand was too, for keeping up with new surgical and medical knowledge emanating from Europe.

Less than two months later, the West Coast Times of 7 March announced that at the monthly meeting of the Westland Hospital and Charitable Aid Board, a letter was received from Dr Teichelmann asking for twelve months' leave of absence. The Doctor pointed out that he had been the Board's Medical Superintendent for fifteen years, and Westland was not only commercially isolated, but medically as well. Therefore he considered it his duty, not only to himself, but to the public, whose servant he was, that he should revisit the centres of medical and surgical knowledge in Europe.[36]

On 22 March 1912, a representative gathering of townspeople assembled at the Hotel Westland to farewell Dr Teichelmann. Nine speakers paid tribute to the Doctor's service to the West Coast. There were countless toasts and a number of musical items, including the ladies singing 'La Marseillaise' in French. He left Hokitika three days later for a twelve month visit to Europe.[37]

On his return the Christchurch Press of 17 January 1913 ran two reports on his journey. One was entitled 'Progress in Surgery', the other 'Among The Swiss Alps'.

He journeyed to the Old Land primarily to bring his knowledge of surgery and hospital work thoroughly up-to-date. After spending a short time in England, he went over to the Continent, and there visited several of the leading hospitals, and attended the sixth Annual Gynecological [sic] Congress, held in Berlin from the 9th to 13th September.[38]

---

35. Ces Preston, personal conversation, September 1993.
36. West Coast Times.
37. Ibid.
38. Christchurch Press, 17 January 1913, p7, col 7.

During his trip to Europe Teichelmann climbed in the Swiss Alps

The reports give details of other visits to hospitals in Berlin, Dresden, Leipzig, Vienna and Birmingham. In Vienna he enjoyed an opera or two, and the medical highlight of his trip was the month he spent at his old hospital, the Birmingham General. Everything that modern science could supply was there, and in order to give some idea of the general thoroughness of the arrangements, he stated that at this hospital the air could not enter the operating theatre until it had been sent through fibrous filters.[39]

When Germany refused to respect Belgium's neutrality, Britain declared war on 4 August 1914. In terms of International Law, the Declaration of War automatically meant the whole Empire was at war. Westland was a world away in distance, but not in terms of culture and blood ties to Mother Britain. This posed some difficulties for Teichelmann, as he had blood ties to both sides in the conflict, through his Scottish mother and German father. There was no doubt where his loyalty lay, but the prejudices of others would have an impact later on.

He had been a member of the 1st Westland Rifles since February 1907 as Captain Ebenezer Teichelmann, and he had been promoted to the rank of Surgeon Major in the New Zealand Medical Corps with the 13th Canterbury Regiment in September 1907.[40]

'In the isolated peace of South Westland you were in danger only if you chose to dice with nature. But on the continent of Europe from 1914 on human-created

39. Ibid.
40. *The New Zealand Gazette*, 19 September 1907.

dangers dominated all else. Because New Zealand's population was then predominantly European origin, this country was deeply involved in the European war, politically and emotionally,' wrote Jim Wilson in his biography on Dr Teichelmann's close friend, Alec Graham.[41]

Major Ebenezer Teichelmann enlisted for service despite being 55 years of age at the outbreak of war. His offer to serve overseas was not immediately taken up by the New Zealand Army, which frustrated him. Although age may have been a problem, it is likely his name and German ancestry were key factors. The British Royal family had changed the name of the House from Saxe-Coburg-Gotha to Windsor, German sausage was renamed luncheon sausage, and people thought to be German were victims of assaults and their shop windows were smashed. Out of frustration and a sense of duty, Major Teichelmann wrote to the British War Office offering his services. On file are a number of letters he wrote to Hon. James Allen, Minister of Defence, trying to hasten his call up for overseas service. Below is one such letter:[42]

Hamilton St
Hokitika
June 7th 1915

Dear Sir -

I beg to thank you for your replies to my letters and trust you realize that it was only my desire to do my duty to my country that inspired me to communicate with you on the subject. At the same time I hope you will not oppose my application to the British War Office should the matter be referred to you.

I am

Yours sincerely
E. Teichelmann

To The Hon. James Allen
Wellington

---

41. Alec Graham and Jim Wilson. *Uncle Alec and the Grahams of Franz Josef.* John McIndoe. 1983, p143.
42. Capt. E, Teichelmann-War Records, McKerrow Collection, Hokitika.

On 25 August 1915, Major Teichelmann was called up in the Medical Corps and assigned to the Sixth Reinforcements with the rank of Captain and number 3/884A.[43] The medical report for that date records his age at 56 years and five months of age. His height was five feet seven inches, and his weight 152 pounds.

He sailed 'privately' about 16 September 1915, according to his record of service, and on 9 October 1915, joined the No 1 Stationary Hospital at Port Said, Egypt.[44] The hospital had been established for three and a half months. Soon after his arrival, the hospital received word that they were to proceed to a 'certain destination near the sea and with a mild, equable climate.[45]

Ebenezer Teichelmann boarded H. M. T. S. Marquette, a ship carrying troops comprising the 29th Divisional Ammunition Column, with its transport and animals, 36 nurses of the New Zealand Army Nursing Services, and a number of other medical personnel from the New Zealand Stationary Hospital. The ship left Alexandria on 19 October, and took a devious course towards Salonika (now called Thessaloniki) in Greece, in the hope of eluding submarines.[46]

Four days later, as the *Marquette* entered the Gulf of Salonika in the Aegean Sea, a young New Zealand nurse was walking on the top deck with friends. They huddled inside their coats, waiting for the sun's warmth. As they walked she glanced overboard and noticed a straight, thin, green line in the water and heard a distinct swishing sound. It was less than fifty metres away and heading directly at their ship. She watched horrified as the *Marquette* was hit. It took seven minutes for the ship to sink.[47]

Chaos ensued. Few of the lifeboats were launched successfully. The list to port resulted in some lifeboats emptying their passengers into the sea. Some boats landed on top of others. Few survived intact, and many people swam until they were exhausted and drowned. Others clung to debris and upturned life boats. Drowning mules and horses added to the watery carnage.

---

43. Ibid.
44. Ibid.
45. Lieut, H.T.B. Drw NZEF (ed). *The War Effort of New Zealand*, Whitcombe & Tombes, 1923.
46. Ibid.
47. Ibid.

One of the New Zealand nurses clinging to a piece of wreckage describes the scene.

> 'I swam about for hours, but as I had crushed my arm between the boat and the ship somehow or other I was feeling very sick and sore. I really did not mind much what happened. …I saw some men hanging on to wreckage, and called to them … and they said it was no good, there were already too many there. Then one of the crew saw me and came along to me with a piece of board, to which I clung for some time. Then he said to me, 'Look out, sister, there is a shark right behind you, paddle for your life.' I did so, though I'd rather drown than be eaten by a shark…'

They eventually reached a partially submerged boat where several others also sat. Every five minutes, the boat would roll, tipping its contents back into the sea. It took until late afternoon for them to be rescued. During this time her rescuer had succumbed to cramp or exhaustion, and died.

> 'Sister Rae came up afterwards, hanging to the lifebuoy of one of our New Zealand boys. She asked me if she could come into the boat. I said, "Yes, sister, but … this boat keeps turning turtle…" She held out for a while, but soon after showed signs of exhaustion and died. I wondered if I should be the next. Men died on all sides. Some lost their reason and went away from us all.'[48]

As Teichelmann clung to his life in this watery drama it is likely he thought that the *Marquette* may have been sunk by cousins, nephews, distant relatives or friends from his father's native Germany. The war was now very real and the stupidity of European fighting European must have hit home. After several hours in the water, he survived the ordeal. Others weren't so fortunate. The death toll revealed that 170 lives were lost following the sinking of the Marquette, ten of the 36 New Zealand nurses and 22 of other ranks in the NZ Medical Corp lost their lives.[49]

The destination, Salonika, was founded about 300 BC and named after the half-sister of Alexandra the Great, Thessaloniki. On 8 November 1912, Salonika, with a Turkish

---

48. Ibid, pp90-93.
49. Ibid, p106.

army of over 20,000 men, surrendered to the Greek Army. In 1915 the present population was 180,000, of which half were Jewish, one fifth Greeks, one fifth Turks, 10,000 Bulgarians and the remainder Europeans and others.[50]

If having survived the icy wintry waters after a shipwreck wasn't enough, now came the risk of being stabbed to death on dry land. Teichelmann, along with his New Zealand colleagues, was billeted in the city, which was greatly congested with several divisions of Greek troops, three French and two British Divisions. The streets were thronged with people from different nationalities and tensions were high. German and Austrian officers were among them. The Greeks were not happy being overwhelmed by so many foreigners, and a number of British soldiers were stabbed.[51]

Lembet Camp - Greece - 1915

A few days later, the unit moved out to Lembet Camp about five kilometres away where the French and British were camped. On 12 November, the New Zealand Stationary

50. Ibid. p105.
51. Ibid. p107.

Hospital established itself, and by the end of November had acquired large marquees for patients, and was well set up to receive the increasing number of war casualties from the front line near Dorian, and later from Gallipoli. Unfortunately, the weather at the end of November was atrocious with strong winds, sleet and snow. It was this blizzard which swept over Gallipoli and caused so many casualties. A few days later the hospital received a number of severe frostbite cases. 'The men stated that they had been standing in trenches with water over their boot tops, and that during the blizzard their blankets and great coats had been frozen rigid.'[52]

Teichelmann's knowledge of cold injuries gained from his years in the high alps of New Zealand served him well. It was a far cry from his work on the West Coast of distant New Zealand where he had a modern operating room to do his surgery. The operating theatre was in a marquee on a raised wooden floor with a strong incandescent light to operate under. Numerous operations were performed by Captain Teichelmann and his colleagues. Surrounding the marquee was a slit trench, and nearby were dugouts to shelter from enemy attacks. All water had to be carted up to the tents. Apart from treating war injuries, accidents and hundreds of cases of frostbite, there were large numbers of soldiers to be treated for typhoid, para-typhoid, dysentery and trench-fever.

As the Allies retreated, the front line moved closer to Salonika and the number of casualties increased. Enemy planes bombed the medical camp on 30 December, and to prevent further bombing, staff painted a large red cross, 30 yards by 20 yards, on each side of the ridge on which the hospital was situated.

The following day, the German, Austrian and Turkish consuls were arrested in Salonika and were put on a French warship because the allies "regarded the bombing of Salonika as a violation of Greek neutrality and as an act of war".[53]

Eight days later the camp was severely bombed causing a number of casualties, and again early on the morning of January 31st 1916, a Zeppelin dropped bombs on Salonika and a few hit Lembet camp.

While working in Salonika with the wounded from Gallipoli, the son-in-law of his

52. Ibid. p109.
53. Ibid, p.110

elder sister Charlotta, Lieutentant Mark Kennedy of Australia's 26th battalion, was fighting in Gallipoli, and sadly died later in 1916 in France, leaving behind a son he had never known.[54]

On 3 March 1916, the No 1 New Zealand Stationary Hospital was relieved by the No 1 Canadian Stationary Hospital. The New Zealanders sailed for Port Said on 7 March. Here the unit staffed the NZ Stationary Hospital, with 600 beds, on a promenade facing the Mediterranean Sea. Surgery was done in the American Mission School building, and outside the marquees accommodated the less severe medical cases and convalescents.[55]

Ebenezer Teichelmann's wide-eyed interest in culture, philosophy and history was being well stimulated. He reveled in humanity in all its guises, and had enjoyed his year among the Greeks, Turks and Egyptians. On 2 July 1916, he was temporarily attached to the 2nd General Hospital at Havre (Le Havre) in France.[56]

Shortly before he arrived in France two New Zealand friends of his from the Maori community of Bruce Bay on the West Coast were creating history. They were Butler Te Koeti and Dave Bannister. Butler had worked as a mountain guide with Peter Graham at Mount Cook in 1905. Nine of this extended Bruce Bay family were fighting in this war. An unofficial World Wood chopping Championship was held in Niepe Forest in France, on April 9, 1916, and the reigning world champion, serving in the Canadian Army, challenged the best axe men in the British Empire.

The world champion was not to know that two Maoris had been chopping all their lives for a living, and for competitions. The crowd was stunned when the brash Canadian lumberjack was beaten. Butler was first and Dave second.[57]

While moving from Egypt to France, verbal salvos were being fired at him thousands of miles away back in New Zealand in an incident which went all the way to the Prime Minister. It was unfortunate that during World War I, excessive patriotic fervour sometimes led to suspicion falling on people with German-sounding names. Dr Teichelmann fell

---

54. Wm. Bruce Kennedy, op cit p. iii
55. Lieut H.T.B. Drew, op cit. pp113, 114.
56. Ibid.
57. A.A. Pullar, *Wilderness Days in Bruce Bay*. Self-published 1990.

victim to this when the Member of Parliament for Grey Lynn brought his name, along with others with German names, to the House of Representatives in June 1916, as a German suspect.[58] This was the type of ill-informed patriotism based on paranoia that Teichelmann abhorred. His commitment to medicine was based on his love of humanity.

An indication of the respect that Dr Teichelmann had earned among West Coasters is revealed through the following incident. Back in 1905, he had come into conflict with a prominent saw miller over environmental issues. That man, George Perry, was later to become the Mayor of Hokitika. Despite the differences in their beliefs, while the Doctor was serving his country overseas, Mr. Perry took exception to the attacks on the likes of Teichelmann, and sent a statement to the Prime Minister:

> "Dr Teichelmann has been for twenty years a citizen of this town and is widely known and respected. He is a British Subject, and the Council of which he was a member deeply resents the action of the member for Grey Lynn in bringing Dr Teichelmann's name before the House in the list of German suspects, and regards his action as an insufferable insult to the town and district.[59]"

In reply, the Prime Minister said that he would be pleased to comply with the Council's request and have the resolution read on the floor of the House.[60] It is likely that this attack on Teichelmann was kept from him at the time.

Two months later on 25 September, Dr Teichelmann was 'detached to England' and joined the New Zealand Medical Corp and served at the Hornchurch Convalescent Hospital. It accommodated 2,500 patients and focused on rehabilitation.

> 'Each man was given the necessary massage, medical electricity, remedial exercises, or such other treatment as was deemed suitable. From Hornchurch the men were transferred to Command Depot Codford to be rendered fit again for service.'[61]

At Hornchurch where the patients were divided into medical, surgical and massage

58. Ron Fields, op cit., p80
59. Ibid. pp80, 81.
60. Ibid.
61. Lieut H.T.B. Drew. op cit. p 125.

categories, he took great interest in studying aspects of rehabilitation for wounded or frostbitten fingers and hands, and he was often called upon to do corrective surgery.[62]

A welcome break from the intensity of surgery was riding on the back of a motorbike with his former climbing partner from the 1901-07 era, the Rev. Henry Newton, and exploring the English countryside. Like his climbing, Newton still had a sense of daring, sometimes bordering on recklessness, as both Teichelmann and later, Alec Graham verified, when motor-cycling with the 'loose Cannon'.[63] After three weeks at Hornchurch, he was transferred to Codford Depot, which might have been better named the Boot Camp, as it marked the return journey to the trenches for those recovering from illness or injury. Situated in the bleak, bare and undulating downs of the Salisbury Plains it was an unpopular place. After convalescing, soldiers 'instinctively rebelled against a return to the front, to the filth, the exposure, the racket of guns, and probable death.'[64]

The 'Boot Camp', Codford Depot, Salisbury England

62. Dorothy Fletcher, personal conversation and notes in Teichelmann file.
63. Ibid.
64. Lieut H.T.B. Drew, op cit. p266-7

Even the somewhat sanitized version of the 'War Effort of New Zealand' acknowledges that Codford had its "lead-swingers" - the black sheep, and that the officers sent here were those who could handle all ranks with tact and consideration. Having roughed it with some of the world's toughest goldminers of all nationalities on the West Coast of New Zealand, Teichelmann seemed quite at home here.[65]

New Zealand Hospital Ship Maheno

However, his stay was short, as competent surgeons were required on the New Zealand Hospital Ship Maheno, and he returned to New Zealand, caring for patients, arriving on 19 December 1916. The Maheno had eight wards and two operating theatres, an anesthetist, sterilizing and X-ray rooms, a laboratory, laundry and drying room, steam disinfector, dispensary, telephone exchange and two lifts, each which could carry two stretchers at a time.[66]

---

65. Ibid. ps127-128
66. Capt E. Teichelmann-War Records, McKerrow Collection, Hokitika.

Teichelmann with war medals

Captain Ebenezer Teichelmann's war record was credited with serving 461 days overseas and forty-five days in New Zealand, making a total of one year and 140 days serving with the New Zealand Expeditionary Forces. He spent three weeks in Wellington staying at the Bowen Street Private Hospital until being finally discharged from the army on 11 January 1917.

On returning to New Zealand he found that a number of fellow mountaineers had died, among them Jim Dennistoun, whom he was quite close to.

Teichelmann was almost 58 years old on his return to Hokitika.

Instead of feelings of joy at his return after nearly one-and-a-half years overseas, it was a time of sadness. His old friend Dr Herbert MacAndrew died on 15 January 1917.[67] Teichelmann and MacAndrew were not only colleagues in medicine, but they played a key role together in the Westland Institute, which was a forum for discussion, debate and being updated on the world at large. In addition, they were great supporters of the Museum where MacAndrew had been honorary curator since early 1900.

Three weeks later Dr Teichelmann was one of the speakers at the farewell for West Coast members of the 26th Reinforcements heading for Trentham, thence to the war in Europe.[68]

The ending of hostilities in Europe was overshadowed by the 1918 influenza

67. West Coast Times.
68. Ibid.

epidemic. As early as September of 1918, there were indications that a major epidemic was taking place in war-torn Europe. No one thought or even considered that this would eventually take as many lives as those lost on the battlefields.[69] Even Dr Teichelmann had time off recuperating from an unspecified, severe illness, and brought in a locum to replace him. He returned to work on 30 September 1918, and resumed his professional duties.

News of an expected allied victory in Europe filled the newspaper headlines from the beginning of November and over the next few days West Coast communities would prematurely celebrate the ending of the war. Children certainly didn't mind the half day's holiday given to them, even if it was by mistake.

By 6 November, men who were due to depart for Burnham camp were instructed not to leave because of the influenza epidemic in Canterbury. From here on, the Hokitika Guardian tells of the events of the influenza epidemic:[70]

> **November 8:** an advertisement asked for women, not necessarily practical nurses, but with some nursing experience, to volunteer for nursing in the Auckland district. The government would pay ten shillings per day plus travel expenses.
>
> **November 13:** a number of influenza cases reported in Hokitika.
>
> **November 14:** a meeting held in the Town Hall to call for volunteers to assist in any way to help mitigate the effects of influenza. An inhalation chamber opened in the Drill Shed in Wharf Street from 2-4 pm and 7-9 pm. Inside the chamber people would be sprayed with sulphate of zinc. It was of no use whatsoever, but kept morale up a little. Another inhalation chamber was opened in the local library in the Carnegie building.
>
> **November 15:** with Dr Teichelmann as overseer, Westland Hospital was soon crowded with patients, so a further twenty beds were prepared at the Victoria School in Hampden Street. The town was divided into blocks, with able men, Boy Scouts and such like to check on houses in their area. Women were asked to help nurse

69. Hokitika Guardian, West Coast Times.
70. Ibid.

patients and look after families of those stricken with the illness or cook meals for the hospitals. Hotels and boarding houses were asked to supply bedding, bedsteads and furniture. Appeals were made for old calico for sheets.

November 19: with thirteen deaths already in the town, St Mary's Club Rooms became a third hospital. The Sisters of Mercy had been nursing the sick since the outbreak began.

November 20: a final year medical student was sent from Dunedin to help Dr Teichelmann, but he caught the flu on arrival and became a patient at the hotel in which he was staying. (Named Billcliffe, he left Dr Teichelmann's private hospital to return home on 7 December). Another Doctor was sent.

November 23: shops which had been closed started opening for two hours a day. Among the other places closed were hotels, schools, churches, places of amusement and barbers and hairdressers. People were not allowed to congregate unnecessarily.

November 25: Dr Teichelmann goes to Ruatapu on a motor jigger to attend the one dozen cases there.

November 26: he visited Arahura Valley to attend severe cases at Humphrey's Gully.

December 7: the epidemic was about over and the auxiliary hospitals closed as patients were being able to be nursed at home.

During the two and a half weeks in which the influenza epidemic raged, 27 local people died. Four women died while nursing the sick, one in the Victoria School Hospital.

Another interesting character came into Dr Teichelmann's life in 1919 - David Ziman. A small man born of Jewish parentage in 1862 in a small village in Russian Poland, (later Lithuania), Ziman's life was nearing an end when he moved to Westland from Reefton in 1919. Ziman had single-handedly revitalised the economy of Reefton, pulling the town out of a 15 year recession with his daring mining ventures.

As a boy, his family had emigrated from Lithuania to England, where he sold goods on the streets of London. Later he made big money from buying and selling ostrich feathers, despite his poor education. He speculated the proceeds on South African gold mine shares, amassing a fortune through his business skills. Then he lost it all and was declared bankrupt, but he recovered and paid off his debts. By the time he arrived in New Zealand on a holiday he was reasonably wealthy again.

David Ziman, in front wearing cap

Ziman arrived in Reefton in the prime of its boom mining quartz for gold in July 1895. He brought to Reefton the dual attributes of mining experience and financial astuteness, and had soon bought several mines, one of which was at Humphrey's Gully near Hokitika. He also speculated in land, and at one stage owned what is now the suburb of Thorndon in Wellington. After 23 years of involvement with various gold mining ventures in the Reefton district, Ziman turned to his old friend Dr Teichelmann for help in his last days:

'Time was running out for David Ziman. His health deteriorated. It seems that his last days were spent close to Hokitika at the gold locality of Humphrey's Gully, in which had earlier shown an interest. Nearby Westland Hospital was the main reason for his presence in the district. There, as his diabetic condition worsened, he was lovingly cared for by Ebenezer Teichelmann, who had been Surgeon-Superintendent since 1897. On 30 July 1920, David Ziman went into a diabetic coma from which he did not recover.'[71]

He was thrilled when Elsie Cameron came back to Hokitika in 1930, at the start of the Depression. She had moved to Nelson in her early teens and was fortunate in securing a job as nurse in Hokitika's Westland Hospital during the Depression.[72]

'I remember him calling out in the ward quite often, "Where's Elsie?" in a squeaky voice, and I just wanted to curl up with embarrassment. He really was quite fond of me,' recalled Elsie Cameron (Davidson).

'He was a most particular man when it came to giving anesthetics; you could never get the temperature right in the flask for him - very meticulous.

'The staff respected him, although they called him Old Teichy behind his back,' said Elsie.

After his retirement and into his seventies, the Doctor's part-time work at the hospital was mainly as an anesthetist. Dr Teichelmann always used a 'shipways' for administering anesthetics, which is now on display at Shantytown, near Greymouth.

The Doctor was renown for his quick replies, often with an acidic barb to it. Ces Preston recounts one incident when his neighbour called the Doctor when she had a sore throat. She had a reputation as a large, voluble woman who thought herself rather above the rest of society. In Ces's words, she was 'twenty stone class'.[73] He examined her, listened to her complaints, and diagnosed laryngitis. The prescription was for salt and water several times a day.

Rather taken aback at this, she asked the Doctor, 'Will this cure me?'

'It cures corned beef, so it should cure you,' he replied.

---

71. Darrell Latham. *The Golden Reefs*, Nikau Press, 1992. p396.
72. Elsie Davidson, personal conversation, June 1993.
73. Ces Preston, personal letter, 7 September 1993.

Horses were the only means of crossing rivers.

Over many years of interviewing people on the West Coast from Haast to the Arahura Pa, nearly everyone the author met born before 1930 on the West Coast had a Teichelmann story to tell. The hundred or so people in this category I interviewed were either "delivered by him", "operated on by him on a kitchen table at the Fox pub at Weheka," or "saw Teichy after I did my knee in playing rugby," "he stitched me up after the mine accident," or "he was rude to my mother when I was sick, saying the child is not the problem, rather the paranoid mother," or "he put my leg in plaster when I fell off a horse".

And then there was Blossom. Carl Hende, a rugged West Coaster, was the ferry man at Hende's Ford on the Wanganui River, north of Harihari. Carl's horses were the life blood of his work and one day, his favourite horse 'Blossom' became lame after injuring her leg on a tree stump. Exploiting the fact that Teichelmann frequently used Carl's horses to ford the river, he wrote a letter saying, "Blossom is badly injured and may die, please come quickly and perform surgery on her. Can you make sure it doesn't cost more than 'ive Pounds." Within 24 hours the Doctor arrived and performed surgery and traveled outh to treat human patients. Blossom lived out her natural life.

In spite of the growing use of x-rays, and common use of antiseptics, Teichelmann ad a struggle to combat old ways. Most people carried on as they always had, going only) a Doctor when all else failed. Home cures were based either on herbal remedies, castor il, tonics, so called old wives' tales, or the private use of such hard drugs as paregoric and pium. Newspapers advertised Stubbs Fern Ointment, which was guaranteed to heal heumatism, sprains, colds and influenza; and Charles' B41 pills could be furtively taken or urinary or venereal diseases. Holloways Pills, Beechams Pills and Davis Painkiller helped eal with any other complaints. Any recent advances in medical practice had to be proven 1 the community before they won acceptance.

Diseases that claimed many young lives over the years the Doctor worked on the Coast were measles, scarlet fever, whooping cough and tuberculosis, along with epidemics f typhoid and diphtheria. On top of those, Dr Teichelmann also had to deal with umerous mining and saw milling accidents. It was a wild and unforgiving frontier, and ie isolation of patients from medical centres meant even more tragedies than today. Too ften help arrived too late. Travel was slow and cumbersome; frequently dictated by the veather. Medicinal supplies were poor, and access to consultation with peers was difficult. ut despite all these impediments, Doctor Ebenezer Teichelmann endeavoured to do the est for his community with the available resources. He made numerous difficult and angerous journeys in the face of ridiculous odds, on the chance that there was still omething that could be done. The lifestyle took its toll on his personal life. He had to attle with self-doubts when lives were lost. But this was a man that sacrificed much for ie sake of his fellow citizens, no matter who they were. Many people owe him their lives.

Social Involvement

As the nineteenth century drew to a close, Teichelmann had mastered a large slice of available medical science. His quest for knowledge continued unabated as he expanded his horizons with photography, horticulture, conservation, public health, peoples' banking and free public libraries. He also worked hard to ensure others had access to knowledge, education and opportunity. But standing out like the Southern Alps on a frosty West Coast morning was his new love, mountain exploration. This became a major feature of his life for the first quarter of the new century. But despite all his medical and surgical commitments, as well as his frequent alpine expeditions, Doctor Ebenezer Teichelmann still found time for his conservation work, the establishment of the Carnegie Free Public Library, other philanthropic and charitable work, and numerous other community involvements.

Looking through the West Coast Times in 1907 reveals Teichelmann's name almost daily. He was vice-president of the local amateur swimming club, president of the Joint Library Committee, a director of the West Coast Times newspaper, a member of the Hokitika Harbour Board, a member of the Hokitika Golf Club, and an officer of the Hokitika Cricket Club.

He was listed on the committee of the Westland Institute on 17 January 1899. Provincial Institutes, or Philosophical Societies, came under the auspices of the New Zealand Institute and its Act, 1867, and served the promotion of art, science or other branches of knowledge. Many Provincial Institutes ran libraries, museums or other institutes of science, art and learning. In the Abstract of the Westland Institute's 1900 Annual Report, Dr Teichelmann is listed as vice-president and the report highlights their work:

The library, being the mainstay of the society, has been receiving the most attentio this year, over one hundred volumes having been placed on its shelves, all of the moder and attractive literature, and a further supply has been ordered, whilst it is in contemplatio to compile and shortly publish a full catalogue. The public reading-room has been kep well supplied with papers, and is largely patronised.

Alongside the Doctor in the Institute were the eminent Dr MacAndrew, who ha got his B.M in Edinburgh, and G. J. Roberts the famous surveyor, and many other of th town's leading philanthropists, scientists and philosophers. Together they sought to enhanc the literary opportunities of Westland.

Towards the end of 1905, the Westland Institute received word from Mr Andre Carnegie that he would grant the sum of two thousand pounds for a new library. This wa a concrete step towards the fulfillment of a dream that Dr Teichelmann had lobbied an worked hard for. Fund-raising had taken several years before the construction could begi and then it was over 30 months for the ornate building to reach completion. Early i 1907, the President of the Joint Library Committee telegraphed the Hokitika Saving Bank to express the gratitude of the committee for the grant of four hundred pounc towards the building costs.

For some time, the doctor had witnessed the slow construction of the library, as was sited directly opposite his surgery in Hamilton Street.[74] Like an expectant parent, h frequently checked on progress when he had a spare minute.

A dream became reality for Dr Teichelmann and a number of his Westland Institu colleagues on 24 June 1908, when the Carnegie Free Public Library was opened. Th building was impressive. An imposing portico supported huge pillars at the main entranc welcoming visitors through swinging doors featuring delicate Murmanese stained glas Unique circular fanlights in coloured glass topped the large double windows, which allowe light to stream through the reading rooms, divided by an ornamental archway. Mantelpiec of carved rimu adorned the fireplaces and rimu dado embellished the walls throughou

---

74. At date of publication it is the Teichelmann Bed and Breakfast accommodation house.

But more important than the building was the grand selection of books, journals, periodicals and newspapers housed inside.[75]

The Carnegie Free Public Library - Hokitika

After Dr Teichelmann addressed the large gathering at the opening of the new library, he called upon Mr. H. L. Michel, the Mayor of Hokitika, to declare the building open. Mrs. Michel unlocked the doors with an inscribed gold key donated by Mr. W. M. Arnott, the contractor. This was a proud day for Hokitika and South Westland, for it brought an institute of knowledge to a scattered population in a remote corner of New Zealand.[76]

Westland's isolation, whilst attractive in its rawness, occasionally led to other problems. As a Doctor greatly interested in Public Health, Teichelmann had become frustrated by the lack of an abattoir in Hokitika. Since the first gold rush in Hokitika in

75. Dorothy Fletcher, personal conversation.
76. West Coast Historical Museum.

1864, meat had been an important part of everyday diet. With thousands of miners flocking to the area, a large number of cattle and sheep were killed regularly. Some years later the cattle disease pleuro-pneumonia broke out at Woodend in North Canterbury and the government placed restrictions on the entry of animals from infected foreign ports and districts. The butchers and diggers of the West Coast protested strongly about these restrictions, as it reduced their meat supply.

> Prior to these restrictions Hokitika's ocean beach presented an awful scene as the flotsam and jetsam of the rivers and tides lined the high water mark; timber from the back woods, wreckage from the once proud ships on the sandbanks, rubbish from man's inhabitation and long lines of offal thrown out from various slaughterhouses along Revell Street.[77]

H. Basting's drawing for the Hokitika Abattoir, 1913.

---

77. Ron Fields, op.cit., pp31-32.

The Government passed the Abattoirs and Slaughterman's Act 1894, and later the Slaughterings and Inspection Act 1900 compelled those boroughs with populations over 2000 to construct an abattoir. What should have been a simple and straightforward matter became a protracted and bureaucratic wrangle as the choice of a site had to meet approval of the Hokitika Borough Council, the Butchers' Association and the Department of Agriculture. The debate on the abattoirs dragged on for well over ten years and during this time the importance was seen 'of having proper provision for the killing and inspection of meat.'

At one stage, Dr Teichelmann led a deputation to the Council with a petition signed by 450 citizens and ratepayers.

Finally, on 1 August 1914, the abattoir was opened by the Mayor of Hokitika, Mr George Perry, and Hokitika at last had meat that was inspected and safe.[78]

Ebenezer and Mary Teichelmann somehow also found time to be great hosts. Photographs from that era show the Teichelmanns at picnics, garden parties, and the opening of public facilities. It seemed their door was always open. He was a close friend of G. J. Roberts, Chief Surveyor for Westland, and Mr. 'Explorer' Charlie Douglas was a regular caller when he was in Hokitika. Mountaineers such as A. P. Harper, W. A. Kennedy and the Graham brothers frequently visited the Teichelmanns. Alec Graham recalls returning from Christchurch with his brother Jim in 1907 and popping in to the Teichelmann's. 'We had a most interesting evening looking over the photographs he had taken on our recent trip to Fox. We also talked over plans for his next holiday. He told me he had practically decided that our next trip would be up the Waiatoto Valley,' writes Alec Graham.[79]

Although Mary and Ebenezer Teichelmann had no children of their own, Mary's name and memory was carried on through Mary Kelly of Woodstock, born in 1900.

> "My great-grand parents were going to name their next child Ebenezer if it was a boy and Mary if a girl," said Paul Madgwick, grandson of Mary Kelly. "I recall her saying 'I'm pleased I was a girl. Mary is a better name than Ebenezer!' "[80]

78. Ibid.
79. Alec Graham & Jim Wilson, op. cit.
80. Paul Madgweck. Hokitika, personal conversation.

Ruera Te Naihi

About this time two boys were born on the same day: to the Whileys and the Davidsons. The fathers were keen to name one of the boys after the great Doctor. The toss went Ebenezer Whiley's way and he was known most of his life as 'Ebe' Whiley, while the other was named Malcolm Davidson.[81]

Jack Bannister, the late Kaumatua (chief) of Te Koeti Turanga Runanga, the tribal group of South Westland, recalled the visits of Dr Teichelmann to his grandfather's house in Hokitika.

"I moved from Bruce Bay to Hokitika when I was a small boy to live with my grandfather, John William Bannister. John Bannister married Hera Te Koeti. Dr Teichelmann used to come round regularly and my job was to fill his pipe and to look after him," said Bannister.

When Teichelmann had a day off or was on holiday, he would stay a lot longer and Jack Bannister said, "Not only did I have to look after his pipe, I had to bring the water to put with the gin that he and grandfather enjoyed now and then. They always drank square gin," recalls Jack Bannister. "We all looked forward to his visits and the time he spent with us.[82] As a frequent visitor to the Maori settlements of Bruce Bay or

81. Ces Preston, personal conversation, September 1993.
82. Jack Bannister, personal conversation.

Makawhio (Jacobs River), he had great admiration for our people and their ways," said Jack Bannister.[83]

He found an affinity with the Maori of South Westland. A number of them were legendary mountain men and guides, such as Butler Te Koeti who accompanied the great English climber Edward Fitzgerald in 1895; Ruera Te Naihi (Bill the Maori) who accompanied Charlie Douglas and Arthur P. Harper on South Westland explorations in 1894; George Bannister, who did the twelfth ascent of Aoraki Mt. Cook in 1912; and Joe Fluerty, the first person to climb Mount Tasman from the west in 1932. In them, he obviously identified with their exploratory spirit.[84]

The Doctor would pop in to the Red Lion Hotel from time to time to have a whisky after work. A young baker delivering bread to the pub remembers the Doctor clearly:

"I always went to the bar to get the money, and this day Dr Teichelmann walked in and he asked for a whisky," recalled Ces Preston. "He had the whisky bottle on the counter and he also took out a little pouch of bitters. He held the glass and shook the bitters in, turned the glass round and then put the whisky and soda in afterwards."[85]

Hospitality was one aspect that most people recall when discussing Teichelmann. He enjoyed entertaining friends and visitors. Often young climbers passing through Hokitika would drop in to meet the Doctor and he would always take them out for a good meal at one of the local restaurants. Alec Graham struck hospitality of a different kind when he spent time in the Westland Hospital in the early thirties suffering from goitre. When he came to leave, he couldn't find his clothes. On inquiring he was told that Dr Teichelmann had taken his clothes to his house and hung them up, so they would be in good condition on his discharge. It is also believed that the Doctor had an inkling that the rugged Graham, who had a dislike for hospitals, might discharge himself early and Teichelmann knew he wouldn't return to Waiho in his pyjamas.[86]

---

83. Ibid
84. NZAJ, 1991, Maori Mountaineers of South Westland, Bob McKerrow.
85. Ces Preston, op cit.
86. Ibid.

February 1917 signaled 20 years since he and Mary arrived in a raw, rough and ready Hokitika. In the past ten years motor transport became prevalent over and above the horse.

On 18 July 1911, the once totally isolated communities of South Westland were changed forever when the first motor car motored south of the Mikonui River. The 20 horsepower Reo Four owned and driven by W. J. and P. H. Renton, drove from Hokitika to Franz Josef in 11 and a half hours, with the actual traveling time being six-and-a-half hours. It was a rough trip as each of the four tyres was punctured.[87]

The first car in reach Waiho (now Franz Josef) in 1911.

87. Graham Collection and Dorothy Fletcher personal conversation.

The use of the telephone and visits to the movie were now commonplace.[88] Teichelmann must have felt a sense of pride for his adopted town and his beloved Westland.

On his return from the war, his mind was still on the horrors of Gallipoli, Somme and Flanders. He put considerable time helping raise funds for the troops still fighting in Europe. Horticulture was another great love, whether it be trying to identify and photograph the native flora or experimenting in his large garden in Hokitika. His reputation as one of the best gardeners in Westland meant his bulbs were greatly sought after, so he gave a selection of his choice bulbs to the Patriotic Committee who had been canvassing for gifts for a mystery parcel. The parcel was raffled and the money used to buy gifts to send to the troops.

Jimmy Cum

The manager of the Kaniere Gold dredge, Mr Ford, won the parcel and handed it to Jimmy Cum, the Chinese Cook at Keller's Hotel (later the Westland) who thought the bulbs were onions. Some days later Dr Teichelmann met Mr Ford and asked him what he did with the bulbs he won. "Oh, I gave them to Jimmy Cum the cook, who said he used them in the stew."[89] Later, Mr Ford went back to Keller's Hotel and asked Jimmy for further details about Teichelmann's choice garden bulbs. "Oh, I put them in the stew; they cooked up very well, and no one complained. They must have been O.K," he said.[90] It was a wonder no one complained about the bulbs in the stew, particularly in light of the regular dose of manure they had received.

88. West Coast Times.

89. West Coast Historical Museum.

90. Ibid.

Jimmy Cum went away one time to Christchurch and he was delayed coming back, so he sent a wire. "Jimmy Cum come when he can come signed Jimmy Cum," recalled Hazel Kelly, whose grandfather owned the hotel and employed Jimmy Cum.[91]

Dr. Teichelmann liked Jimmy Cum and would often take a half hour every so often to talk with him.[92] Chinese, Lithuanian, Maori, Estonian, Irish or whatever, he really loved diversity in the true sense of the word.[93] Coming from Jack Bannister meant something as he was a Maori from South Westland and had a Korean wife and lived in Asia many years.

The secret to Dr Teichelmann's great flower garden and prized bulbs lay with Mr J. Cameron, the local general carrier, who used his team of horses to pull tip drays for sand and gravel from the local beach and rivers. The potent concoction for the Doctor's garden came from the very middle of Mr Cameron's stable. When the horses were put away for the night, they would feed from chaff boxes on the wall, and the horses would mostly pass urine in the middle of the stable, and Ebenezer always wanted this for his flower gardens. The centre of the stable would always be kept separate for flower gardens. The men who delivered the urine-soaked manure always said: "The stink was terrible, but Teichie always had a wonderful flower garden."[94]

Although Teichelmann was elected to the Alpine Club (England) in 1903, he didn't become a member of the New Zealand Alpine Club until 1914, when the club came out of recess.

In 1920, the Doctor found time to help the New Zealand Alpine Club get back on its feet again. The New Zealand Alpine Club had been founded in 1891 and 'the Club, in the years 1891 to 1896, was able to hold frequent and regular meetings, an annual dinner, and now and then an exhibition of photographs.'[95]

But as members became more scattered, the club became dormant. In 1914 a general meeting was held in Wellington, the rules were amended and new officers elected. The war intervened and little happened in the club until 1920. Arthur P. Harper was elected

91. Hazel Kelly, personal conversation.
92. Ibid
93. Jack Bannister, personal conversations, 1992-93
94. West Coast Historical Museum.
95. NZAJ, 1921, p6.

President, G. E. Mannering Vice-President and the committee comprised Malcolm Ross, Hugh Wright, Dr J. K. Inglis, T. N. Broderick and Dr E. Teichelmann. The Hon. Secretary-Treasurer and Journal editor was T. A. Fletcher.[96]

Although Teichelmann put some time into the New Zealand Alpine Club, a lack of time was the single factor against him making further forays into the mountains. In the 1922 NZ Alpine Club Journal is an article of his, 'The Pioneer Pass.' In his introduction Teichelmann writes:

> Not having the leisure just at the present time to write a full account of the explorations at the head of the Fox Glacier, carried out by the Rev. Mr. Newton and myself in 1903 and 1904, I forward you an article on 'Pioneer Pass,' published in the Auckland Graphic Christmas Number. The proprietors have kindly given their permission to reprint it. I would only ask readers of the journal to remember that it was written more than eighteen years ago, and not especially for climbers.[97]

He held various offices in the club including President in 1936-37 and Chairman of the Canterbury-Westland Branch in 1936-38.

Transportation was beginning to change the face of Westland and on August 1923, the first train went through the Otira tunnel, connecting the West Coast to Canterbury by rail. The Otira tunnel claimed the distinction of being the longest tunnel in the British Empire at that time, five miles and 554 yards.[98]

It was now possible to travel from Greymouth to Christchurch in less than half a day. This suited Dr Teichelmann, who had to make frequent trips to Christchurch and Wellington for medical conferences, New Zealand Alpine Club meetings, Acclimatisation Society and conservation business, and of course, to give lectures.

Although the train removed the last vestiges of isolation from Central Westland, it was the aeroplane that was to have the greatest effect in reducing the remoteness of South Westland. Dr Teichelmann was to play an important part in convincing people of the worth of the aeroplane.

---

96. Ibid.
97. NZAJ, 1922.
98. Grace Adams. *Jack's Hut*, A.H. & A.W.Reed, 1968

Otira Tunellers 1918

However, he is best-remembered in this era for being on the first flights over the Franz Josef Glacier. Flight-Lieutenant Maurie Buckley brought his Avro 504K to Hokitika by rail, introducing hundreds of people to the thrill of flying during the Hokitika Exhibition. When Buckley decided to make his historic trip south to the glaciers, there was only one volunteer: Dr Teichelmann.[99]

Strange to say, not one other person could be persuaded to make the flight. As luck would have it, Havelock Williams, a Timaru photographer, arrived at a crucial moment.

"Now then, Lock," said Buckley, "you are just the fellow. We want some pictures, and we start first thing in the morning."[100]

99. Leo White, *Wingspread.* The United Press Ltd, Auckland. pp 64-65.
100. Ibid.

Visibility was poor on the next morning, 23 January 1924, so they waited until the afternoon, setting off south at 4.50 pm. Dr Teichelmann describes the trip:

> "In ten minutes we were over Lake Mahinapua, but to the seaward of it, the tailings of the Rimu goldfields and the various tracks and roads in the district being prominent to the subjacent landscape. Ross looked pretty in its little hollow. The mouth of the Mikonui was next passed, the Baldhead Road, the tramway to the Waitaha River and the Main South Road showing very distinctly as bright streaks in the bush... We were now flying very high, and immediately beyond the big Saltwater Lagoon, near the mouth of the Wataroa River, the Okarito Lagoon showed up very plainly. As we rose higher it became colder, and we appreciated the warm head-gear and goggles that we had been advised to take with us. The Saltwater and Okarito Lagoons were crossed at an altitude of 5000 feet, and the pilot then turned inland, rising all the time. Lake Wahapo was passed over on our left. Lake Alpine and Lake Mapourika were immediately under us, and we got a glimpse of the Graham's Hotel at the Waiho.[101]"

Teichelmann was obviously spellbound, seeing the land he had walked, ridden and climbed over during the past seventeen years. At Waiho (now Franz Josef) there was a special moment as the plane approached. "From one of its windows peered the quizzical face of Ebenezer Teichelmann, and the next moment his hand came out and attempted to drop a little parachute intended for Mr Graham."[102] The parachute, bearing a message for the Grahams, got caught in the tail, then dropped off, but it was never found. Teichelmann was pleased to see the glacier he knew so well from the ground.

> "...the Franz Josef became more and more a prominent feature, and from an elevation of 6,200 feet the steep descent of the great river of ice became noticeable. It was a grand sight...
>
> "At an elevation of 6,300 ft we crossed the lower spurs of Mount Moltke and the snout of the glacier, making back directly for Okarito. A landing was made on the beach south of the mouth of the Okarito River.[103]"

---

101. Lyttelton Times, 25 January 1924.
102. Ibid.
103. Ibid.

Before the first flight over the glaciers in 1924. (Dr. Teichelmann on the left)

As the plane came in to land, Doctor Teichelmann had his chin resting on the edge of the cockpit and was totally absorbed in the splendid scenery. 'Williams, realizing that landing among fairly big stones on the beach might mean a jolt sufficient to break the good Doctor's jaw, dropped his camera and pulled the Doctor back, just in the nick of time.'[104] With overcast weather and darkness approaching, Maurie Buckley decided to stay the night in Okarito. The aircraft was pushed back to the pub and anchored down for the night "where everybody was jubilant at the success of the flight."

In the morning, it was found that the night high tide had rendered the beach too rough to take off from. After searching the area for a suitable strip, Captain Buckley

104. Alec Graham & Jim Wilson, op cit. pp160-161.

settled on a large mud flat bordering on the Okarito Lagoon. The local people helped Buckley, Teichelmann and Williams wheel the aircraft over the sand banks and through the town to the old wharf. From here local ingenuity was needed to get the plane across the lagoon to the mudflat. An old pontoon belonging to the port was located and the plane loaded on and floated across the lagoon. It was a delicate operation requiring a lot of skill, and made difficult by encroaching darkness. Once across Captain Buckley wasted no time getting the Avro airborne and forty-five minutes later landed in Hokitika after an historic flight.[105]

Biographer Jim Wilson described the significance of this flight, which he says 'created a new order for the Coast as a whole... In the years to come, light planes landing on beaches or on strips prepared in paddocks were to revolutionize travel on the West Coast, and are today in a host of ways, vital to the tourist business.'[106]

Teichelmann found the experience of flying delightful, and could see its future uses for surveying and science:

> 'There is something mean about inspecting country from the air. It is like taking the roof off a house and watching the performance from above. I should say that to the experienced eye it would yield up most of its secrets. I felt I could almost tell the nature of the soil of the different parts of the country passed over. Heavy timber, light timber, flax, swamp, Pakihi and lagoons could all quite easily picked out. Nothing was more distinct than the desolation produced in the sawmill areas that have been cut out and subsequently fired - such as between Hokitika and Ross and around Lake Mahinapua.'

Having assisted surveyors in the past, Teichelmann predicted the importance of the future use of planes for aerial surveying. 'The aeroplane, coupled with photography, should save the Survey Department much expenditure.[107]

As his retirement fast approached, Dr Teichelmann looked at ways he could continue to serve his community.

---

105. Lyttelton Times, op cit.
106. Alec Graham & Jim Wilson, op cit. p68.
107. Lyttelton Times.

Since arriving in Hokitika, Teichelmann had seen so many married working men squander their money on drink or gambling and it was often through their wives and children coming to him as patients, that he could see their suffering. It was something he discussed with the Graham brothers on trips into the mountains and later as they became senior leaders in their communities.[108] He believed that accessible Savings Banks would create an environment for thrift. The minutes of the Hokitika Savings Bank Trustees meeting on 30 March, 1926 'resolved Dr Teichelmann be appointed to represent the Hokitika Saving Bank at the International Conference of Savings Banks to be held in Philadelphia in October next.' He had been a bank trustee since 1921 and regularly attended meetings.

Defiance Hut on the edge of the Franz Josef Glacier

The Right Hon L. S. Amery, a British Cabinet Minister who was Secretary of State for the Dominions, paid an official visit to New Zealand in November-December 1927. Being a keen mountaineer and skier, he desired to cross from Mount Cook to Franz Josef Glacier, via Graham Saddle. With Peter Graham as his guide and accompanied by the President of the New Zealand Alpine Club, Arthur P. Harper, his daughter Rosamond, and Peter Graham's nephew Dave, they climbed the two peaks of the Minarets and Mount de la Beche and crossed Graham Saddle on 9 December, and then on to Defiance Hut. The next day, 10 December, 1927, they walked out to Waiho. 'At Waiho we were met by Peter's brother, Alec Graham, and by another great pioneer of New Zealand, Dr Teichelmann, and spent the next day peacefully at the Graham's comfortable Hotel.'[109]

108. Personal conversations, Peter McCormack and Dorothy Fletcher.
109. The Rt Hon. L.S. Amery, C.H., *In the Rain and the Sun*. Hutchison & Co Ltd., 1946. p153.

S.S. Jane Douglas 1909

Maori Community at Bruce Bay 1909

Before departing New Zealand from Auckland, Amery had 'some discussions with the New Zealand Alpine Club about the need for more and better mountain huts' and final talks with Coates, the New Zealand Prime Minister. This is a fascinating comment because the only lack of a decent hut that he encountered was in the vicinity of the Almer Glacier area where 'we got to the remains of the old Almer Hut and brewed some tea.' They reached Almer bivouac early evening, and were almost benighted on the Franz Josef Glacier en route to the lower Defiance Hut.[110] Less than two years later there was a spacious new Almer Hut. Obviously Amery had lobbied successfully about mountain huts.

Towards the end of 1929, local body elections were held in Hokitika. Dr Teichelmann put his name forward for the Hokitika Borough Council and the Hokitika Harbour Board. The Doctor's popularity in town was evident. Of the ten people who stood for election, the Doctor polled second with 859 votes, only 1 behind D. J. Evans, the highest poller. He polled the highest with 839 votes in the Harbour Board elections.[111]

Why was standing for the Harbour Board so important? "Teichelmann had worked in the remote parts of South Westland in communities like Bruce Bay, Jackson's Bay, Haast, and to reach these places overland by car, horse, it could take four days or even two weeks, depending on the state of the rivers, as to whether you could cross them or not."

"By ship, these remote communities often with large Maori populations, could be reached in an overnight journey," said Maori chief, Jack Bannister. "Teichelmann cared for our people, people whether they were European, Chinese or Maori."[112] Dr, Teichelmann could see that by regular shipping schedules to Jackson's Bay, a natural port, that natural resources could be selectively culled and exported. He coined the phrase sustainability before it was popular, a term he bought back from Switzerland in 1912 where he saw communities thriving on a combination of tourism and judicial use of natural resources in a sustainable manner.

110. Ibid.

111. West Coast Historical Museum.

112. Jack Bannister, Personal Conversation, 1992

Conservation

It is difficult to be a mountaineer and not succumb to the seductive call of the wilderness. It is difficult to be a good photographer with no sense of aesthetic beauty. It is difficult to be a skilful surgeon without experiencing the wonder of the human body. Ebenezer Teichelmann was no exception. Whether or not his concern for the preservation of the wonders of nature came before or after his outdoor experiences is unimportant. He was far-sighted enough to take an active part in the protection of special places from the ravages of unbridled greed. He sought to protect its beauty for future generations and to capture on film for the benefit of others some of the joys of the wilderness that he experienced.

Conservation is an emotive word in Westland, and has been for several generations. Since the first sealers established a fur export industry in South Westland and Fiordland, the balance of power has favoured the human 'conquerors'. Colonization involved subduing the wilderness: replacing jungle, the habitat of the devil and savages, with the pasture and lawn of Arcadia; clothing and proselytising the heathens; and extracting the wealth from the natural resources for the good of the empire or the church, no matter what the cost to the environment. For some, it was important to 'conquer' the peaks. Nature was a horse to be broken in and harnessed. Very few people imagined that this horse might get old or sick, or even need a rest occasionally. Even today, many Coasters regard it as their right to treat the environment as they see fit. Even the natural attractions are regarded as revenue generators rather than there to be loved and nurtured for their own sake.

Teichelmann's love of South Westland is understandable and obvious. The huge legacy of superb photographs he has left reveal his commitment to this area. The Doctor also took a keen interest in Lake Kaniere, Punakaiki and the Arthur's Pass regions. Later he became very active in the formation of scenic reserves and National Parks in these areas to ensure that their alluring beauty could be appreciated well into the future.

But he was no greenie activist intent upon locking away resources forever. When his varied involvements are examined, it is apparent that he had a vision for the future generations of New Zealanders. The places of outstanding beauty should be protected from the ravages of civilization, but be available to be experienced in perpetuity by anyone who wished to enter on nature's terms. Practical by profession and personality, he appreciated that society cannot exist on aesthetics alone. A beautiful view does not satisfy the stomach. Sustainable management of the resources was the key to survival.

Although Dr Teichelmann loved the bush and was at heart a conservationist, he believed that some lowland areas of South Westland held promise for further cattle farming and logging. He met with the executive of the Canterbury Progress League in Christchurch on 20 December, 1924, to discuss the potential he saw in the Okuru area. In introducing him, the chairman Mr A. F. Wright said, "There was no greater authority on South Westland than Dr Teichelmann."[113] During his presentation, the Doctor explained how Jackson's Bay was a natural harbour, and that it would provide access to and from this remote part of South Westland.

About 1900, Teichelmann had become a member of the West Coast Acclimatisation Society. He went on to become its president, and in that became involved in several projects, such as the establishment of salmon hatcheries at Kaniere. It is unclear what stand he took when on 15 March, 1907, the Society received word from the Tourist Department about the proposed liberation of chamois in Westland. They had been presented by the Emperor of Austria.[114] Had he known of the future cost of introduced species, he undoubtedly would have opposed their release.

Teichelmann was not one to be intimidated by the might of others, and he even crossed pens with the powerful timber industry. On 29 September 1905, he was clearly upset by a letter written to the editor of the West Coast Times. George Perry, later the Mayor of Hokitika, was the owner of a major sawmill. A circular from the Commissioner

---

113. Hokitika Guardian, 22 December, 1924.
114. West Coast Times, 15 March, 1907.

Lake Kaniere

of Crown Lands to sawmillers intimated that no more sawdust could be deposited in streams or lakes. If this practice persisted legal proceedings would be taken against them. Perry protested against this decision, and mentioned that a petition was being prepared to evidence the extent of the opposition to this move. With the industrial and political smugness typical of local body politicians he stated: 'I have no doubt it will receive the cordial support of the vast majority of the people of the district'.

Teichelmann's reply in the West Coast Times the next day was far from cordial.

> '... there is no necessity why sawmilling should be conducted as to be destructive to any other industry. Sawmillers have no right to pollute streams than any resident in this town has the right to run sewerage on to his neighbour's land... What is done in other countries in this matter? Does Canada or the United States permit the pollution of streams by sawmillers? Certainly not; the sawmillers in those more up-to-date countries consume their own sawdust in the furnaces and thus save fuel - at the same time getting rid of the nuisance'.

He went on in his long letter to defend the position of the Acclimatisation Society which had been attacked in the paper's editorial the previous day.

> 'I am not a fishing man; and never caught a trout in my life, but I hope someday to see freshwater fish as a source of food supply, and whitebait not the only canning industry on the Coast. Your leading article of the same date is written in much the same strain as Mr Perry's letter and I would only call attention to and object to your stigmatising the work of the Acclimatisation Society as intended to contribute purely to the pleasure of people. No part of its work is primarily intended for the production of pleasure, and there is no more strictly utilitarian society existing than this. Because it is slow in producing the desired results it is only the thoughtful who realize the great good which must ultimately accrue from its disinterested action.'[115]

Four days later Teichelmann received support from an unexpected quarter. In a telegram to Grey Valley sawmillers regarding the disposal of sawdust, Richard John Seddon, the Prime Minister said: 'The Land Commissioner is only carrying out the law and it is a matter in which I cannot interfere.'[116]

Seddon could and did interfere in any matter he chose. Apparently he shared Teichelmann's vision of a West Coast largely unpolluted and unspoilt by human mismanagement.

As his interest in botany and photography grew, he built up a friendship with the eminent botanist, Dr Leonard Cockayne of Christchurch. An important result of their early collaboration was a report in 1915 on indigenous vegetation on the Port Hills above

---

115. West Coast Times, 30 September, 1905.
116. West Coast Times, 3 October, 1905.

The following people were nominated for a period of five years: The Mayor of Hokitika, The Chairman of Westland District Council, The Commissioner of Crown Lands for the Westland Land District, The Conservator of Forests for the Westland Forest-Conservation region, Dr Ebenezer Teichelmann, David John Evans and John Noble Robinson.[129]

At the first meeting on 8 October, 1934, a ground committee of Dr Teichelmann, S. C. Darby, Conservator of Forests and J. N. Robinson, was appointed to report in regard to matters for attention at Lake Kaniere.[130]

Lake Mahinapua

The first annual report of the Board shows a far-sighted and hardworking group. They cleared large areas of blackberry, erected notice boards regarding fire control, the destruction of flora, swimming and water pollution; and appointed honorary rangers. They were among the first in New Zealand to express concern about the effects possums, stoats, weasels and rats were having upon native birds. They voiced their concern:

129. Ibid.
130. Ibid.

'The decision of the controlling department to discontinue issuing permits to trap opossums on scenic reserves had caused the Board some concern as it is considered that trappers are responsible for the destruction of much vermin of these reserves such as stoats, weasels and rats. Moreover from enquiries made it is ascertained that the damage done to bush on scenic reserves by trappers is almost negligible, and it is more than favourably offsetted [sic] by the destruction of vermin mentioned which are the natural enemies of our native birds.'[131]

Teichelmann's involvement in the Lake Kaniere Scenic Reserve Board grew in its first three years, and it became a very effective nature preservation body, but at the same time encouraging recreation. The Doctor's experience from serving on the Arthur's Pass National Park Board was proving invaluable to steering the Kaniere Board in similar directions. Both reserves today are substantially attributable to the vision of this man. Here was a fine example of one man making a difference.

Doctor Teichelmann was a man with a belief in the preservation of nature for the benefit of all people. But his convictions did not exist solely in the purchase of a few glossy photography books to show visitors, or even the membership of a conservation organization. He lobbied and fought unselfishly for those long term goals. He suffered hardships to explore and record those wonders for those who did not have the means to access the wilderness. He was a man who lived what he preached. Bruce Watson, a former Conservator for the Department of Conservation, West Coast Conservancy, acknowledged the difficult pioneering work achieved by Teichelmann. "In an era and region where national resources were often exploited with scant regard for posterity, gaining protected status for Arthurs Pass, Lake Kaniere, Lake Mahinapua, Punakaiki, later the Paparoa National Park, and the four glacial Scenic Reserves of South Westland, later Westland National Park, was a tremendous achievement."[132]

---

131. Ibid.
132. Personal Conversation, Bruce Watson

Mentors : G. J. Roberts and Charlie Douglas

As the Medical Superintendent of the Westland Hospital, Ebenezer Teichelmann's responsibility was to provide medical services from the Taramakau River 25 kilometres to the north, to Jacksons Bay 350 kilometres to the south. Most of South Westland was classified as 'Charlie Douglas country.' This was the hardy Scot who was fascinated by unexplored valleys, wild bush, untrodden mountain peaks, and glaciers issuing icy water into rivers that charge through gorges, some still impenetrable to people. Almost a legend, Charlie Douglas spent the major part of his life living under a bat-wing tent with only his dog for company. He surveyed and mapped unknown and feared parts of South Westland. Shortly after the new Doctor arrived in Hokitika, local papers announced that the Royal Geographical Society had awarded 'the Gill Memorial Prize to Mr. C. E. Douglas for his persistent explorations during twenty-one years of the difficult region of forests and gorges on the Western slopes of the New Zealand Alps.'[133]

It was on or under these same western slopes that Teichelmann spent the remaining 41 years of his action-packed life, many in the footsteps of Charlie Douglas.

In 1897, Ebenezer Teichelmann was 37 years old and in peak fitness. Charlie Douglas was 57 and was physically slowing down, and his boss, G. J. Roberts, at 49 years of age 'was confined to office work, but the memory of his surveying among the mountains remained as a lasting influence.' Both the older men suffered deteriorating health from

---

133. John Pascoe, *Mr Explorer Douglas*. A.H.& A.W. Reed, 1957. p57.

constant hardship and deprivation during long and arduous survey trips. Years of rough living - in damp clothing, sodden boots, monotonous diet, prickly woolen singlets and shirts, leaky tents, weeks of incessant rain and energy sapping damp and cold, loneliness, isolated for days by flooded rivers, impenetrable gorges and bush, being constantly bitten by mosquitoes and sandflies, and wiping ones backside on leaves and ferns - had taken its toll.

Charlia Douglas (left) with Andrew Scott

The relationship between Roberts and Douglas is central to understanding the history of mountain exploration and surveying of South Westland, and the sub-conscious influence the pair had in putting exploratory fire into Teichelmann's belly.

Roberts and Douglas made a good pair. Both became totally absorbed in Westland

and its mountain mysteries, and could not tear themselves away, despite the wider opportunities they could see elsewhere and the failings they observed in the Coast as a community. Both were retiring personalities, but full of quiet good humour. Roberts described their relationship as one between 'two good human beings who fully understand each other and, ignoring our many weaknesses, fully appreciate the remainder.'[134]

In 1890 Roberts led the first survey party to venture into the glaciated regions of Westland. To him must go the credit of being the first New Zealand-born mountaineer to read up on the subject of mountaineering beforehand. With his foreman Dan Strachan, he went up the Wanganui Valley to the Lambert Junction, and spent three days cutting a track from the forks up a steep bush ridge to a rock promontory which terminated a range coming off the Divide. This promontory, named Blue Lookout, became central to later journeys by Douglas and Teichelmann who built on Robert's earlier survey. Roberts completed his 1880 explorations by moving from Blue Lookout and exploring the snow grass platforms. 'Above them rose a line of vertical rock faces (the Lord Range) and towards these the party moved, finding the snow slopes very useful for by cutting steps (we) got to the top of peaks otherwise unscalable' until they were 'finally jammed by the western (south-west) precipices of Dan's Peak'. Eventually the party found access to the Main Divide by following along the northern side of the Lord Range to the point where it met The Divide.[135] Here three high massifs met at a low depression (which they named Strachan Pass) leading through to the Ramsay Glacier in Canterbury. Among lower peaks there were potential trig points and, through the pass, others of much the same altitude could be seen in line; both close at hand on the Butler Range and far away on the north shoulder of the Arrowsmiths.'

'Roberts found mountaineering skills to be essential in the course of his work, and had forged a link between mountaineering and surveying.'[136]

Teichelmann struck up a firm relation-ship with these two great explorer-surveyors.

---

134. John Pascoe, ibid.

135. NZAJ, John Acheson, Mr. Surveyor Roberts, XXV1,1973,p 105

136. Trish McCormack, *A History of Survey and Mountaineering in South Westland.* Department of Conservation, Hokitika, 1988. pp23, 30.

G.J. Roberts

During 1900 to 1915 while both were in ill-health leading to their respective deaths, Teichelmann was their medical Doctor as well as close friend. 'The late Mr J. G. [sic] Roberts, Chief Surveyor and Commissioner of Crown Lands for Westland, always took interest in our climbing expeditions, and was helpful in supplying detailed maps and advice,' wrote Teichelmann in the 1923 NZ Alpine Journal. [137] When Teichelmann embarked on his 1908 expedition up the Waiatoto in January 1908, he referred to 'a diary that the late Charles Douglas gave me many years ago,' meaning pre-1908.[138] The influence of Charlie Douglas and G. J. Roberts was strong, but so was the pull of the mountain landscape.

It is hard to break through the reserve of G.J. Roberts but one letter written to John Robert Dennistoun dated 9 September 1908, exhibited rare emotion

Your very interesting and welcome letter of 29th June duly to hand. Will you kindly accept my sincere apology for not replying months earlier. I was away in the N I ill when your letter came there and I have only just got back, you will perhaps pardon a short reply to your letter. All being well you shall have a tracing of the best information in hand of the Wataroa-Godley country, also all we know jointly of the area.

I am delighted with your map, and your account, sorry that you had such a bad time. I don't believe Gunn ever got to (Z) ?. He tells me of getting onto a ridge and seeing

137. NZAJ, Dr E. Teichelmann, 'The Relation of the Rakaia and Rangitata on the East to the Wanganui and Wataroa on the West'. 1923. p169.

138. NZAJ, Dr E. Teichelmann, 'The Waiatoto Valley.' 1935. pp18-24.

a grass saddle- I thus knew he was exaggerating. Glad to hear of Mannering, my best regards to him. Provided you don't adopt names like 'Polly', 'Julia'etc, you may name all unknown country you explore.

Charlie Douglas was spending his winters in Hokitika working on his giant maps of the West Coast until 1905 - "I can picture discussions, with him, Roberts and Teichelmann gathered round one of the huge maps in the evenings, wondering about how to fill in the gaps, " wrote Simon Nathan, a geologist who spent over 20 years on the Coast and knows the huge map well.[139]

Teichelmann greatly admired his friend Charlie Douglas. They met on numerous occasions and Douglas had both confided in and given Teichelmann his diaries.[140] Sadly, Douglas' years of exploration were drawing to a close, while the Doctor was just warming up for his. In the spring of 1906, Charlie Douglas suffered his first stroke while up the Paringa River, and he was carefully ferried by friends back to Bruce Bay, from whence a steamer took him to Hokitika for treatment. While recovering in Hokitika he was given the best of medical care under the guidance of Doctor Teichelmann.

Douglas recovered from his first stroke. In his biography on Charlie Douglas, John Pascoe refers to Charlie staying at Lake Kaniere:

'The Department Report of 1907 has no reference to Douglas, but in January 1908 he was at Lake Kaniere writing to Harper for the last time.'[141]

Ebenezer Teichelmann had lent his holiday house to Charlie so that he could be back in the bush he loved,[142] but Charlie preferred tenting outside.[143] Two local lads playing at Lake Kaniere recall seeing Charlie Douglas on the lake shore looking in reasonable shape.[144] He was camped near Dr Teichelmann's house, quite content to be again among the tall rimu, miro and matai.

---

139. Simon Nathan, personal correspondence, 18 March 2004
140. John Pascoe, op.cit.
141. Ibid.
142. Graham collection, Hokitika.
143. Ces Preston, personal communication. 1993.
144. Ibid.

Lake Kaniere was a haven and a respite for Hokitika residents, who would go there by horse and gig for weekends and holidays. The Doctor preferred to bike out, as it soothed his mind and kept him fit. His friends were important and he enjoyed the company of Donald Cameron from the fish hatchery who would row across the lake to play cards. One day while they were playing cards, "The lake came up so rough, like a sea, that my father had to stay the night with Dr Teichelmann," said Ellen Chesterman nee Cameron. This was some time before 1907.[145] On one occasion when Cameron rowed across to play cards with the Doctor, Charlie Douglas was there.

Later in 1908 Charlie Douglas had a second, more serious stroke. The following year Teichelmann advised Arthur P. Harper that it would be kinder for him not to see Charlie as he would be upset at not being able to talk.[146]

Teichelmann saw to it that Douglas was well cared for. Charlie lived with Mrs. Jane Ward, the widow of Bob Ward who had drowned in 1881 crossing the Omoeroa River. For those who know the Oemeroa it is a seductive valley, a valley that pulls you up. Bob Ward and Douglas had made a number of survey trips together and Douglas had got to know Jane Ward well over the years. Jane Ward lived at 20 Fitzherbert Street, which was either next door to G. J. and Mrs. Roberts, or two houses along from him. It is likely that with his former boss being a neighbour, further support was close at hand. According to Jane Ward's grandson, Tom Ward, Douglas lived in accommodation at the rear of the house.

> "He was a very shy person, particularly with women, but this he overcame with time. His long association with the family meant that he could talk easily with Mrs Ward," recalled Tom Ward.[147]

But G. J. Roberts was not a neighbour for long. He was never able to see the fruits of Teichelmann's more successful 1911 expedition, for he died in Hokitika on 14 September, 1910.[148] Teichelmann was still grieving for his wife Mary, and must have missed his mentor G. J. Roberts, who had encouraged and inspired him to explore remote regions

145. Ellen Chesterman, personal conversation, 19 September 1993.
146. John Pascoe, op cit.
147. Tom Ward, personal letter. 9 July, 1993.
148. John Acheson, op.cit.

of Westland. The death of Roberts must also have been a sledge-hammer blow for Charlie Douglas. Roberts was his closest friend, an explorer- in- arms and boss for so many years.

Teichelmann's cottage at Lake Kaniere where Charlie Douglas camped

On 4 July, 1911, Charlie Douglas was admitted to the Westland Hospital for forty-four days.[149] Here on the hill overlooking Hokitika, with its brilliant views of the Southern Alps, Dr Teichelmann ministered to his old friend Charlie Douglas in hospital. He visited Douglas regularly, and the conversations surely would have drifted to Teichelmann's most recent trip up the Wanganui, and of course to Charlie's explorations in South Westland.

149. John Pascoe, op cit. p66.

There is no record of Dr Teichelmann talking to Charlie Douglas about the recent trip up the Waiatoto, but it would be inconceivable to think that the Doctor would not have had a good yarn about the trip as Douglas had lent him diaries and maps.

Charlie Douglas' years from 1906 until 1916 were painted by historians John Pascoe[150] and Philip Temple[151] as being tragic, stroke-ridden and paralyzed. It is more likely that his final years were warm, comfortable and friendly ones, although he would have had bouts of pain, and the frustration of limited mobility and poor speech. In those final years, Teichelmann was his Doctor and friend; Arthur Woodham, his old mining friend from Waiho, assisted Mrs. Ward in looking after him; and Mr and Mrs. Roberts were neighbours. Duncan McFarlane and his large family were regular visitors.[152]

"Charlie would have been well looked after, you wouldn't have got a better woman than Mrs. Ward. She was so kind, and with her nursing training he would have got good care," remembered Hazel Kelly.[153]

> "Another hospital attendant told me that when Explorer Douglas was hospitalised in old age, the Doctor saw to it that he had his hot toddies at night: his rheumatics played up," said Ces Preston.[154] "The hot toddies were made up of whisky and hot water."

Both Pascoe and Temple claimed Charlie never recovered from his second stroke:

> '...but he was not to recover from the more massive blow which struck him down in 1908. From then, until his death in Hokitika in 1916 at the age of seventy-five, Douglas lay paralysed, unable to even talk with his friends.'[155]

John Pascoe concluded that after the second stroke, 'he never recovered sufficiently

---

150. John Pascoe, op cit.
151. Philip Temple, *New Zealand Explorers - Great Journeys of Discovery*. Whitcoulls, Christchurch, 1985. p163.
152. Dorothy Fletcher, personal conversation.
153. Hazel Kelly, personal conversation, August 1993.
154. Ces Preston, op cit.
155. Philip Temple, op cit.

to roam again in the bush or the ranges.'[156] But he was to roam in the bush again in a limited way, for he was seen walking on the shores of Lake Kaniere in 1911. There the bush came right down to the water's edge.[157] He was neither paralyzed nor unable to speak.

Ces Preston describes meeting Charlie Douglas:

> "I met him through going to the lake with some of my cobbers - I was there with Hector Davidson who was three years older than I. Hec said, "There's Mr Douglas." He had a tent there. I saw him go to the tent and he said hello to us as he passed. The tent had a fly on it. I was told later by a very reliable source that the good Doctor wanted Charlie to stay in his house, but he said, 'Oh no, I want to stay in the tent." That would have been late 1911," recalled Ces Preston.[158]

Ces Preston is clear in his mind that it was Charlie Douglas, for in later life he discussed these boyhood memories with his friend Hec Davidson, and they had no doubt at all that it was him.[159]

What is interesting is that Teichelmann advised A. P. Harper not to come and see Douglas in 1909 after his second stroke 'as he would be upset at not being able to talk to him, and it was kinder to leave him alone.'[160] The question posed is, did Charlie's West Coast friends, Roberts, Teichelmann, Woodham and Macfarlane, close ranks to keep the rather boastful Harper away? Roberts' opinion of Harper was 'how unconsciously full of self' the youthful Harper was.[161]

A. P. Harper, a member of the New Zealand Alpine Club since its inception in 1894 and later president for many years, was likely to be tarred with the brush of disdain Douglas had for 'that gang of amateurs called the New Zealand Alpine Club. They have done nothing and explored nothing that wasn't known long before.' He also said, 'some

---

156. John Pascoe, op cit.
157. Ces Preston, op cit.
158. Hec Davidson (June 1993) and Ces Preston (Sept 1993), personal conversations.
159. Ces Preston, op cit.
160. John Pascoe, op cit.
161. John Acheson, op cit.

crack brained idiot who wishes to make what he calls a record, and whose ambition is to be a small hero in a lecture hall, a drawing room, or even pot house..."[162]

Whilst Douglas' criticisms were in the main directed at Malcolm Ross and George Park, early members of the New Zealand Alpine Club, he and fellow West Coasters held a high degree of distrust and suspicion against the East Coast amateur climbers, who came over and made exaggerated claims about exploits in the west.

> "I believe it is likely that Teichelmann, and Roberts in particular, protected Charlie from Harper," said Dorothy Fletcher, daughter of Alec Graham.[163]

Charlie Douglas's health was failing. He was back in the Westland Hospital from 4 July, 1914, for 34 days, and in again from 5 September for 24 days. On 10 October the same year he was re-admitted, never to leave.[164] While receiving the best possible care and treatment from fellow explorer Ebenezer Teichelmann, Charlie must have felt a sense of accomplishment and peace as he viewed out his window the hills, mountains and land he explored as his life slipped away.

Teichelmann cared for Charlie Douglas as both a Doctor and close friend and various nurses at that time said to Elsie Davidson that "the Doctor always made a beeline towards Mr. Douglas's corner of the hospital when he was there and they would have long talks."

Sadly, Dr Teichelmann was stationed in Port Said when his old friend of a kindred spirit Mr Explorer (Charlie) Douglas died in the Westland Hospital, Hokitika on 24 May, 1916. He was seventy-five years of age.[165] Teichelmann must have regretted not being there to see his friend 'cross the divide', the expression of the era for describing the death of explorers and mountaineers. But during a world war where daily death was the norm, not many people noticed, except his close friends of the land and mountains.

> 'In the wider canvas of a world war his death was minor news in Westland. He became cherished in the memories and writings of his friends such as Harper, Teichelmann, and other mountaineers.'[166]

---

162. John Pascoe, op cit. p78.
163. Dorothy Fletcher, op cit.
164. John Pascoe, op cit.
165. Ibid.
166. Ibid, p68.

Philip Temple in his book New Zealand Explorers says 'It can be argued that Douglas was New Zealand's greatest explorer. Certainly he was the most persistent, the most devoted to the cause of discovery. Early explorers, like Brunner, had sketched in the outlines of New Zealand. Charlie Douglas filled in the last blanks on the map. By the time his work was done, the true exploration of New Zealand was complete; only a few difficult alpine regions remained to be traversed.'[167]

Teichelmann became the key figure in traversing those difficult alpine regions, linking west to east and east to west and completing the work of Douglas and Roberts.

---

7. Philip Temple, op cit. p163.

Cook Valley 1906, waiting till the clouds roll by.

Through The Lens

The art of photography had fascinated Ebenezer Teichelmann ever since he was a young man, and after his arrival in New Zealand he was inspired to compose and record what he saw. When exactly he had acquired the knowledge and equipment is not clear, but by the time he arrived in Hokitika he had both. Strongly in love with the curves and angles of nature, he set about creating a huge collection of images that reveal today the extent of his appreciation of light and shade, form and texture.

Another great alpine photographer and later friend of Ebenezers, Will Kennedy, describes Teichelmann's ability with the camera:

'Though the Doctor possessed a number of cameras most of his photographic work was done with 5 x 4 film and a whole plate camera. The few who now-a-day know what a weighty and cumbersome thing a whole-plate camera is with all its attendant paraphernalia including supplies of heavy glass plates, will understand why the porters (used only on the lower levels) regarded with askance, and tried to dodge those swags containing the heavier parts of this photographic outfit. Yet, that whole-plate camera found its way, in spite of all its drawbacks, up the Franz Josef Glacier to Cape Defiance and on to the summit of Halcombe Peak; up the Fox Glacier as far as the Pioneer Ridge; up the Cook River Valley to near the head of the La Perouse Glacier, and up on to the Balfour Range; up the Waiototo Valley and on to the Therma Glacier; up on to the Sealy Range; and up the Tasman Glacier to the Malte Brun Hut. This camera which he kept to the end of his life reflects much of the finest photographic work the Doctor produced, both alpine and otherwise.

Remarkably fine photographic results were obtained from about the heads of the more southerly sub-tributaries of the Big Wanganui namely the Lord and the Lambert, and from the Divide Peaks of Malcolm, Snowy and Tyndall, and these photographs later proved of great assistance in the mapping of this country.

On the eastern side of the Main Range with the Hermitage as centre, the Doctor did additional fine camera work from the Sealy Range, Footstool, Haast Ridge and Malte Brun Range. Though he ascended Mount Cook (third ascent) via the Linda Glacier, owing to adverse weather conditions no photographic records were taken. From all his alpine standpoints the Doctor made it a practice to secure panoramas as nearly complete as possible.'[168]

The diversity of his photography is illustrated in the *Department of Lands and Survey, Extract From The Annual Report On Scenery - Preservation For The Year Ended 31st March 1930*, written by Dr L. Cockayne C.M.G.F.R.S, and Dr E. Teichelmann, Member of English Alpine Club. There is a selection of nine of his photographs ranging from a close-up of crape ferns to forest and mountain landscapes.[169] Many of his photographs appeared in New Zealand Alpine Journals, various climbing books and were used extensively by the New Zealand Tourism Department to promote the West Coast overseas.

His photographic work was acknowledged publicly by the Chairman of the Westland County Council, Mr W. J. Jefferies, in a farewell speech in 1926: "The Doctor's work in booklets and pamphlets had gone all over the world and he had not spared himself in his efforts to extol the beauties and attractions of Westland."

The mayor at the time, George Perry added, "He had taken a particularly prominent part in advertising the district, especially its alpine attractions. His photographs were excellent and the record he possessed was a tribute to his pluck and skill."[170]

It is quite clear that Teichelmann's photography was a key element in raising public awareness for the early scenic reserve status given to Lake Kaniere, Punakaiki, Arthur's

---

168. NZAJ, 1939.

169. Department of Lands and Survey, extract from The Annual Report on Scenery Preservation for the Year Ended 31 March 1930, W.A.G. Skinner, Govt Printer, Appendix C, 'The Glacial Reserves of Westland.'

170. West Coast Historical Museum, op cit.

Looking across Fox Glacier to Mt. Tasman

Pass and the four Glacial Scenic Reserves that eventually made up the Westland National Park in 1960. Punakaiki (Paparoa) and Arthur's Pass also became National Parks.[171]

But photographic skills do not arrive overnight, nor from reading a book. They are acquired through trial and error. Alpine photography requires a keen sense of light values, and Peter Graham recalled that the Doctor's first attempts on the Spencer Glacier were all over-exposed.[172] Fortunately he learned from the experience and went on to become one of the best of his era.

The Doctor was very keen to see the International Exhibition being held at Hagley Park in 1907, for it contained many of his photographs. At the Hermitage that year Teichelmann was met by Mr Longdon, the director of the British Art Collection, who had travelled to New Zealand to see the exhibition. Longdon was also a mountaineer, and was checking out climbing possibilities whilst in New Zealand. They enjoyed each other's company in the Mount Cook area, before Teichelmann set off to Christchurch for the exhibition while Newton and Graham continued climbing.

Teichelmann's close friend and mountaineer Will Kennedy, some six years his junior, first met Ebenezer at the 1907 International Exhibition in Christchurch where Kennedy had been taken with magnificence of Teichelmann's photography.

> Among the photographic exhibits adorning its walls were displays of many whole-plate photographs of Westland scenery bearing his name. The outstanding beauty and excellence of these photographs attracted my attention so tremendously that I longed to know the man who was responsible for them.[173]

Kennedy was President of the Canterbury Mountaineering Club and an active member of the New Zealand Alpine Club. They shared a common interest in mountaineering and photography. But the Doctor's lack of a system prompted Kennedy to help him.

On one occasion, during one of his many visits to Teichelmann's home in Hokitika,

---

171. *Canterbury Mountaineer*, 1939.
172. Peter Graham, *Peter Graham: Mountain Guide*. Reed, 1973. p40.
173. NZ Alpine Journal, 1939. 'In Memoriam'

Kennedy, always a methodical man, decided to tidy up the Doctor's photographic records by cataloguing them properly. From that day on it was Teichelmann's humorous lament that he could no longer find anything.[174]

Malcolm Peak

When I returned to New Zealand in November 2003 to do some finishing touches to this book, an album of 600 prints of Ebenezer Teichelmann had been recently discovered in a garage in Christchurch. I trembled as I opened this book on Colin Monteath's table in his library as if I was opening a door for the resurrected Doctor. The album was divided into 11 sections and each print was a 5 inch by 4 inch contact print of his large format

174. *Canterbury Mountaineer*, 1939.

negatives. Each photograph had a neat white border around it, with a number and a brief but accurate caption. Who had put this album together? Ebenezer Teichelmann himself, or was it Will Kennedy working with Teichelmann to get his photographs into a tidy collection? One clue is the caption to the photograph captioned Alf Day, followed by a question mark. Day should have been Alf Dale. Teichelmann would never have made a mistake with a name on a fine and much respected traveling companion. Perhaps Teichelmann dictated the captions to Will Kennedy.

Strangely, all the photographs in this album were taken before 1912. Was this the first of a series or a one-off? The album reveals the human face of miners, ferry-men, Maori communities, ships, railway lines, bridges, roads, horses, homesteads, camps, huts, houses, hotels, fellow climbers, waterfalls, river-crossings and rivers, creeks, lakes, gorges, passes, glaciers, ice-falls, hot springs, ice tunnels, and wonderful mountain landscapes. One classic photo is of Dr. Teichelman, in mining clothes and a sou'-wester hat, ready to go down a mine shaft.

Teichelmann's photographs (and Newton) appeared regularly in the Canterbury Times, New Zealand Graphic, Weekly News and the Otago Witness and a stand alone supplement named 'A Tour Through Westland' all between 1902 and 1910.

Dorothy Fletcher has in her collection a large brown album with all the photographs that he and Teichelmann had published, along with a handful of other climbers. This album was sent by Henry Newton and has inscribed in the inside cover, 'Alex Graham in remembrance of old days, Henry E Newton.'

Dorothy said Canon Newton sent it to her father, Alec Graham in the early 1930s.

Newton has made a detailed index of each photograph and story published by he and Teichelmann in his unmistakable handwriting that one gets to know after reading his hand written diaries.

The photographs are a smorgasbord of panoramic mountain centerfolds, small cameos of life in Westland, people, homesteads, ships, valleys, rivers, gorges, mountaineering, a selection of which are in this book.

Montage from NZ Christmas Graphic-1909
Photographs by Dr. E. Teichelmann and Ben Thiem

But not everyone was overawed with Teichelmann's photography. Louisa Graham had to give up the use of her bath-room at Waiho, Franz Josef to Dr. Teichelmann and her husband Alec. It was converted into a dark-room every time they returned from a trip for the Doctor to develop his large 4x5 inch negatives. "This became routine after every major trip in the mountains as Teichy wanted to get the negatives developed as quickly as possible at our house so he and Daddy could enjoy the fruits of their labours after carrying the heavy camera into the high mountains," said Dorothy Fletcher.

One can imagine the

anticipation and excitement that built up in the Graham bathroom as each plate negative was developed, and the results admired or rejected.

Teichelmann was fortunate in having a sound professional photographer in Ben Thiem, who was based in Hokitika. Being a busy professional, Teichelmann didn't have the time to print his own negatives and then mount them on glass to use as lantern slides. So the Doctor used Ben to do quite a lot of his processing work.

Teichelmann taking photo on upper Fritz Range

Sherry Cowie donated a wooden large box of lantern slides to Dorothy Fletcher. In the accompanying note Sherry writes, "These slides were from Ben Thiem, a photographer in Hokitika. My mother, Sybil Turner, worked for him in the 1930s. She got these from either Ben Thiem, or ET (Ebenezer Teichelmann), who was a second father to Sybil." In examining these lantern slides, they would appear to be those taken by Dr Teichelmann and appear elsewhere. However, with the close relationship between W. A. Kennedy, Ben Thiem, and the Doctor, occasionally they would borrow slides from each other, and possibly give each other slides, so they could give more complete presentations.

Impressions as a child are often vivid and accurate, and Dorothy Fletcher recalls the atmosphere when visiting Dr Teichelmann's home as a young girl every time she did a trip to Hokitika with her father, Alec Graham, and it was always the last stop. "He loved to see dad and it was always a warm welcome for him and me. Teichy did all his work in a large, darkish room with a distinctive smell of pipe tobacco," she recalled, as her visits were usually late in the afternoon and the trees would block the sunlight. "He had a big chair, photos on the wall of mountains and people. Cameras, tripods, slide boxes, maps, photographs, books, magazines letters, papers and his pipes were scattered around. "My sister and I were fascinated by his pipes as some of them had little caps on them," recalls Dorothy Fletcher. He wasn't untidy or disorganized, rather a busy man and appeared to have systems for filing and storing.

Dorothy also mentioned that Teichelmann had copied photographs from Buller's Book of Birds to enhance his photographic slide talks.[175]

Teichelmann could count on a number of leading New Zealand scientists as his friends. Among these was Dr Leonard Cockayne the botanist, and Professor R. Speight the geologist. On 13 June 1928, Professor Speight introduced Dr Teichelmann to a full audience at the Christchurch Public Library lecture room. The Doctor's lantern lecture was on 'New Zealand alpine, lake, and forest scenery', which was given under the auspices of the Christchurch Tramping Club.[176]

In a free conversational style, always interesting, Dr Teichelmann described the different slides as they were screened. The majority were of the Southern Alps,

175. Personal Conversations with Dorothy Fletcher, Oct 2003
176. The Press, 14 June 1928. p15, col 3.

their high peaks, great glaciers, and other prominent and interesting features. Especially noteworthy was the series showing Aorangi, 'the cloud piercer,' Mount Cook, from various aspects. For the purpose of contrast they were shown views of the Swiss Alps and of Mount Everest. The views of Franz Josef and Fox Glaciers were especially fine and the combination views of Westland scenery - alps, lake, and forest - evoked warm applause...

Tourism was imperceptibly becoming a significant revenue earner for the West Coast. The jewels in the Coast crown were the glaciers, but tourists would stay at Hokitika, Ross, Harihari or Whataroa en route. In 1923-24 the Hokitika Exhibition was staged, and it brought large crowds to the region. Teichelmann was busy behind the scenes ensuring the exhibition was a success. Many of his photographs were used in promotions and displays.

Ebenezer Teichelmann not only mastered the idiosyncrasies of large format photography, but he excelled with images that extolled the beauties of his beloved mountains and West Coast. His prints were sought after for promotional publications, and the outstanding quality of his large prints with their superb tonal range must rank him among the best of his time. Had he exhibited in North America or Europe, his name would be far more widely known as a photographer.

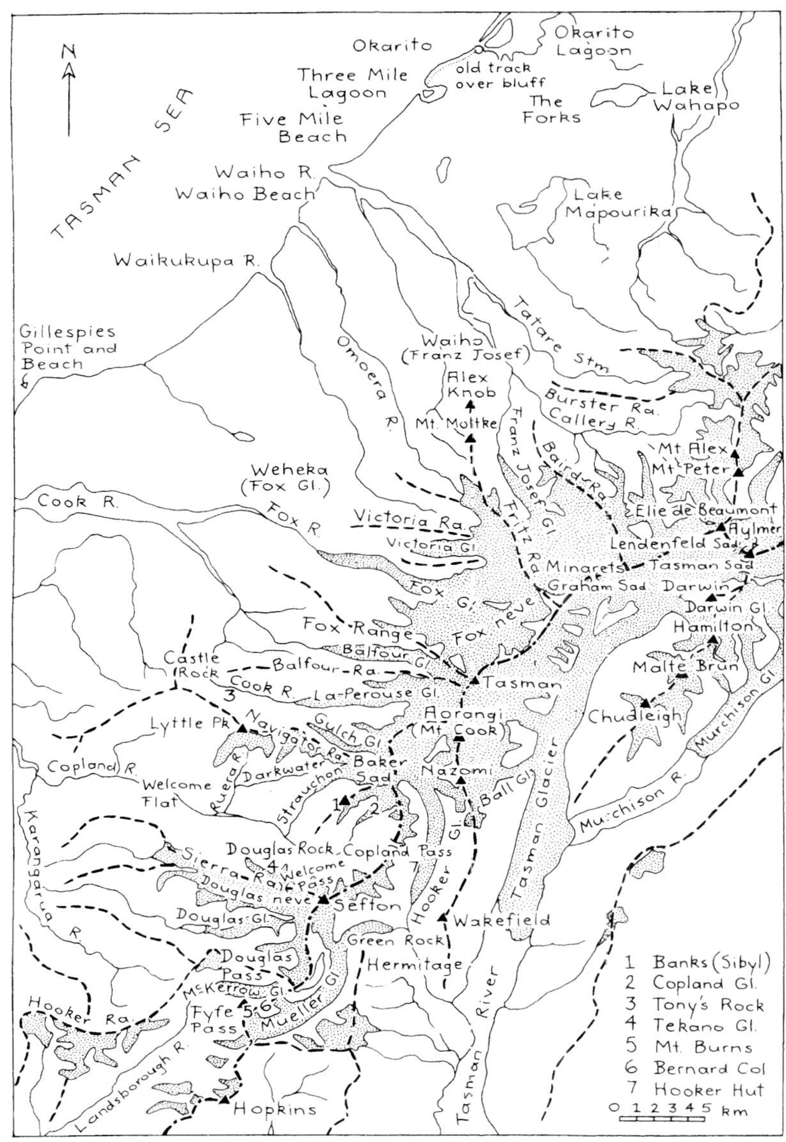

'Teichelmann Country' the Central Southern Alps where he did much of his climbing

From goldmining to Mountaineering - 1899

South Westland has a powerful effect on most people. On a clear day from Hokitika you can see a large number of New Zealand's highest peaks. Mounts Cook, Tasman, Dampier, Torres, Lendenfeld, Haidinger, Minarets and Elie de Beaumont stand out clearly. From his home in Hampden Street, his surgery in town and the Westland Hospital at Seaview, Dr Teichelmann couldn't help but see the high mountains as he moved from home to work and back again. Perhaps the words which describe G. J. Roberts' attachment to the West Coast could equally apply to Teichelmann. 'The love of land is the beginning of nationality, and in the isolation of the West Coast the colonial had found a home.'[177]

The 'Little Doctor', as he was affectionately known to close friends, met many early miners and explorers as he traveled on his far-flung medical forays into South Westland. Men with intriguing nick-names such as Wombat Jack, German Harry, Piggery Charlie, Tony the Greek, Bill the Maori, Harry the Whale and Jimmy Cum from China. Taking an interest in the lives of his patients, and what reasons enticed people from all over to settle in remote parts of South Westland, the Doctor acquainted himself with many varied lifestyles. Like himself, they had been seduced. But many of these characters had not just fallen for the beauty of Nature's charms - they were after her jewellery. It wasn't long before he too was bitten by gold-fever and became friendly with the brothers, Charles and Harold Stoner, and Mr Lee. Sometime in 1899, Dr Teichelmann set up a small gold-mining partnership with these three men.

---

177. NZAJ, Vol XXVI, 1973. p105. John Acheson, 'Mr Surveyor Roberts'.

Early that year Arthur Woodham and Peter Graham had spent three months in the Callery and Burster Range area and had found enough gold to pay expenses and share twenty pounds between them. Further down the Callery at Little Beach, the Friend and Watson party struck it rich and were washing up an average of one pound weight in gold a day, and had three extra men working for them on wages.[178] Teichelmann knew Arthur Woodham as well, and through him had heard of young Peter Graham. Enticed by the adventure of gold, Teichelmann joined the Stoner brothers and Mr Lee in backing the Grahams financially. Their mission was to go back into the Callery late in 1899 to find the elusive mother lode from whence all gold came. Woodham and Graham were paid two pound ten shillings a week in return for a share in what they found.

This business venture led to Teichelmann's first excursion into the mountains. He teamed up with Arthur Woodham, Charlie Stoner and Peter Graham, who were working various gold claims in the upper Callery River. The Callery River is a fearsome valley lying just north of Franz Josef, running between the Baird Range to the south and the Burster Range to the north. It is fed by the Spencer Glacier, draining the Main Divide from Mount Elie de Beaumont along to the Minarets, then up to Drummond Peak, as well as the Burton Glacier, Maximilian Range and the Tatare Range.

There are gorges within its passage that never see the sun, and are reputed to be dark enough to see Venus at noon.

Teichelmann had written to Arthur Woodham, seeking their approval to join them for the purpose of taking photos. Arthur was a genial chap and keen to please, so he replied that he would be delighted to have him along. Charlie Stoner came out to meet the Doctor and took him up to the second, 'Rainy', camp where the rest of the group was waiting. This was Peter Graham's first meeting with the Doctor. He had envisaged a 'great big fellow' of Teutonic proportions, in keeping with his current impression of other Germans he had met. Consequently he was surprised and amused by this quaint, wiry little man with the squeaky voice.

The next morning the party packed up the Burster Range, with Peter Graham carrying

178. Peter Graham, op.cit. p41.

the Doctor's full-plate camera, weighing around twenty-three kilograms. His first stop was to take a photograph of the Spencer Glacier.

> 'While focusing his camera he seemed to be oblivious of everything else, and we had to stand over him lest he put his feet on something which would topple him over. When he had the camera set to his satisfaction he would emerge from behind his black cloth and invite us to have a look. If we approved he would take the picture.'[179]

The party up the Callery

179. Ibid, p40.

Later that afternoon they arrived at Avalanche Camp, which is about one and a half kilometres downstream from the confluence of the Burton Glacier and the Callery River. A fine spell of weather enticed them to camp about 500 metres higher up on the ridge between the Burton and Spencer glaciers, which gave them a base to explore the two remote glaciers. The camp site was on a grassy plateau entirely covered with mountain lilies. The party explored the Burton and Spencer Glaciers and discovered a metre-wide quartz band, but no gold. Teichelmann was in his element and loving every minute of it. 'The little Doctor was greatly interested in this expedition. We had difficulty in getting him along at all as he wanted to take photographs of everything,' wrote Peter Graham some years later.[180]

Young Peter Graham was overcome by the beauty and the remoteness of the area after a full afternoon exploring the Burton Glacier. They had been right up under the north face of Elie de Beaumont, and had witnessed the unusual sight of pink snow. This phenomenon is caused by a vegetable growth, *Protococcus nivalis*. Then the moon slowly rolled up Maximilian Ridge. 'I was so impressed with the wonder and beauty of all we had seen that I just couldn't stay in the tent after our meal but lay outside among the lilies. As the day drew to a close, the lower hills were sharply outlined by the last rays of sun. My vision ranged over a vast expanse of country which I had never seen before from such an angle and my mind seemed to expand with it. The happening of the day crowded in on my thoughts - the beauty of the flowers, the pink snow, the grandeur of the mountains all round - all this, perhaps, not seen before by human eyes.'[181] So overwhelmed was he that he claimed this day was the day of his initial commitment to the mountains. It would be safe to assume that a similar impact was made upon the Doctor, as what had started out as a photo opportunity turned into a lifelong devotion to mountaineering.

Here they spent seven days exploring the Spencer and Burton glaciers before the Doctor had to return back to Westland Hospital. As Dr Teichelmann parted from Peter Graham at the Burster Camp, he said, "You know, Peter, this mountaineering - it's a bug - it 'gets' you doesn't it?"[182]

---

180. Ibid, p41.
181. Ibid, p41.
182. Ibid, p42.

This is a key statement for there is a clear shift from gold prospecting to recreational mountaineering. It really was the birth of modern mountaineering on the West Coast, where people living on the West Coast went into the mountains for the fun of it; exploring and photographing. Teichelmann was 40 years of age when this first trip started him on a 25 year stint into South Westland's mountains. He was hooked. The bug never left him. It similarly marked the beginning of the alpine guiding careers of the Graham brothers.

Mt. Elie de Beaumont towered above them as they explored the Burton and Spencer Glaciers

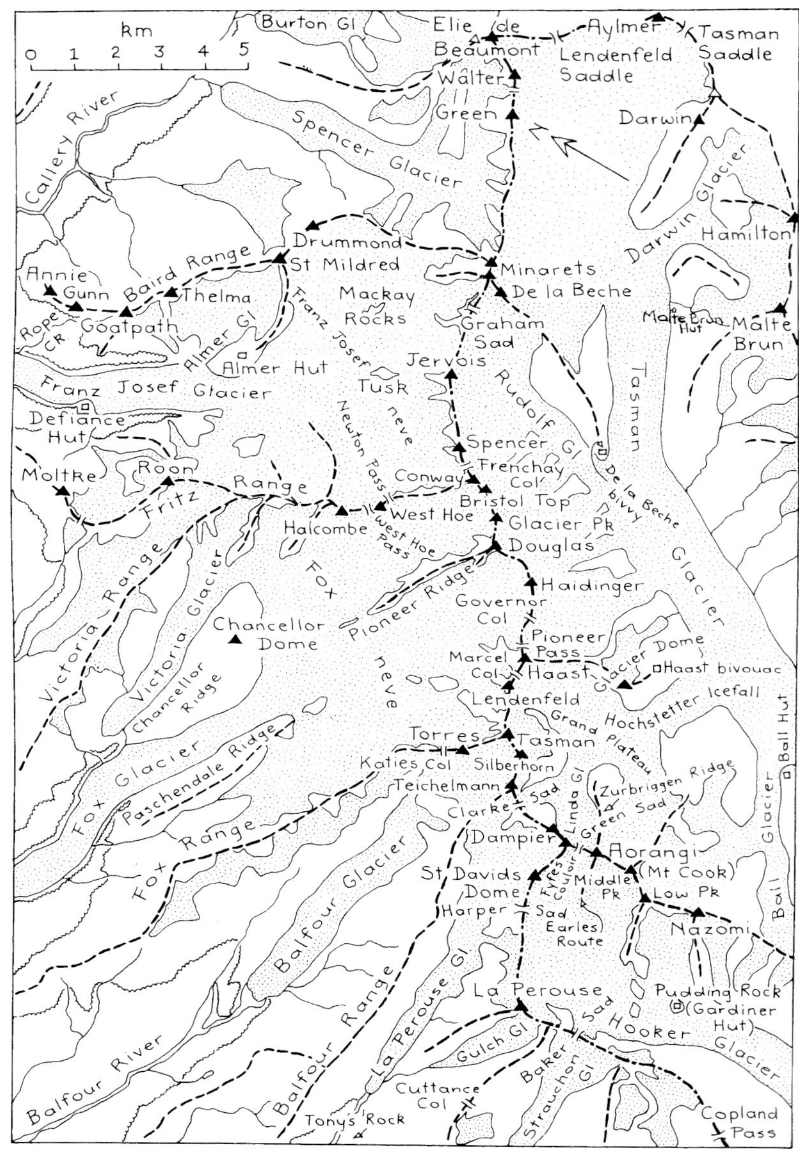

The Franz Josef, Fox and Tasman Glacier regions of the Southern Alps

The Expeditions

1900 Exploring the Fox and Victoria Range

A new century dawned and with it the excitement and prospect of the first real climbing expedition for the Doctor and his friends. In January 1900, he was making plans for a trip into the Fox Glacier region. Unfortunately Peter Graham was working a gold claim and unable to accompany Teichelmann. "Peter, you are deserting me,"[183] he told Peter Graham as he passed through Waiho Gorge. But once Graham had explained the predicament of not being able to walk out on a gold claim, he arranged for Charlie Stoner and Alf Dale of Hokitika to accompany him.

Alf Dale was an ideal companion, as he had gained considerable experience working with Charlie Douglas in the Copland and Whitcombe Valleys, and through doing general track and hut work in South Westland.[184] Alf was no stranger to snow and ice having crossed glaciers, snow passes and saddles assisting Charlie Douglas and, being a miner, like Charlie Stoner, was able to adeptly cut steps in snow and ice with his adapted miner's pick. As we see in the first Newton/Teichelmann expedition in 1902, Newton the experienced mountaineer was impressed with the way another miner and hotel owner, Batson, had used a slasher to cut steps on the journey up to Graham Saddle.

The party set out from the terminal face of the Fox Glacier after a night in an old tin hut situated close by. After spending most of the day on the Fox Glacier, they climbed Craig's Peak. Not a lot was recorded about this trip, but Peter Graham reported that they

---

183. Ibid, p47.
184. John Pascoe, *Mr Explorer Douglas*. A.H.&A.W. Reed, 1957.

traversed the Victoria Range and ascended several peaks, including Mount Purity (1845m). Their intention had been to cross to the Franz Josef Glacier, but when they reached the saddle at the top of the range, the Fritz Glacier was so broken they were prevented from proceeding further.[185]

Alf Dale and Charlie Stoner

It is likely that Dr Teichelmann had a copy of Edward Fitzgerald's book (published in 1896) *Climbs in the New Zealand Alps*, and was following Fitzgerald's map which shows the route over Blackburn's Saddle into the Fritz Glacier and then over Zurbriggen's Saddle into Franz Josef Glacier. It appears Teichelmann's party reached Blackburn's Saddle and descended down to the Fritz Glacier where they turned back.

This was ambitious adventure at its best, for apart from a rough sketch map of the area, and only Fitzgerald and Harper having been there before them, all the high peaks as far as the eye could see, apart from Mounts Cook and Haidinger, were unclimbed.

History was created by this first local West Coast expedition which set out to climb mountains - not for surveying, not for gold - but for the pleasure of recreation and achieving first ascents of Mounts Gaskill, McIntosh, Ferguson, Vickers, Purity and Craig Peak while traversing the Victoria Range.

185. Peter Graham, op.cit. p47.

Reflecting on this milestone, Mike Browne, who has been a mountain guide and running a guiding business for over 30 years out of Fox Glacier, said:

"When you look at the Victoria Range you have to be experienced at route finding and have solid mountaineering skills, and add to that they had, the previous year, climbed up onto the Spencer and Burton Glaciers, and also ascended almost up onto the Maximilian Ridge, I have no doubt that Teichelmann and especially Peter Graham had developed reasonable mountaineering skills before the arrival of the Englishman, Rev. Newton. "

Apart from the aging Stoner and Dale who passed their exploratory skills to the young Graham brothers, Peter and Alec were gaining their own experience on snow, ice and rock. Peter Graham had climbed up almost to the top of the Maxmillian Ridge in 1899 with Teichelmann and derived considerable experience on the Spencer and Burton Glaciers and was living at Waiho, where he was able to get on to the glacier regularly. Once Alec and the rest of the family moved to Waiho in 1900, on most Sundays they would either go onto the glacier for the day exploring ice caves and crevasses and quickly became quite competent at moving on ice using adapted miner's pick axes, or going up the Callery Valley, via the Callery Ridge and then up the Goat Path. Today Goat Path is rarely used as it is a very difficult alpine access route only to be attempted by competent mountaineers and yet they, as young men seemed to run up and down which shows a high level of balance, confidence and fitness. Having lived their young lives on a remote beach, a five kilometre walk from the nearest village round a rocky coastline, the boys were experienced at scrambling over rocks and up cliffs to avoid the incoming tide, as well as climbing trees for fun or looking for bird's eggs.

Goat Path, a difficult access route to the upper Franz Josef Glacier.

1902 First Crossing of Graham and Baker Saddle

Later in 1901 a young Englishman arrived in Westland to take up the position of Vicar of Ross and South Westland. He had told the Bishop that he did not mind where he worked, as long as it was near the mountains. A keen mountaineer, he had developed his mountaineering skills in the Lake District of England, and also was a veteran of five seasons in the European Alps.[186] Alex Graham recalls meeting the Reverend Henry Newton shortly after his arrival in Ross:

He was a young man then, full of energy and keenness, and I noticed while he talked to one and another his eyes often wandered to the mountains.[187]

It didn't take long for Teichelmann with his wonderful grey eyes and Newton with his wandering mountain eyes to team up. Bishop Julius had given Newton a letter of introduction to Dr Teichelmann, 'who, he said, would like a companion to share his mountain trips.'[188]

'Dr Teichelmann and Mr Newton were two very different personalities, but one had a tremendous admiration for them both; to put it simply they were both gentlemen in the full meaning of the word. They both had a good sense of humour, if in different ways; Mr Newton's chuckle over any funny incident was good to hear. Mr Newton was a strong, well built man with boundless energy and an almost boyish keenness when out in the

186. Graham Langton, CMC Journal, 2003 (draft), Ebenezer Teichelmann-Pioneering Mountain Explorer
187. Alec Graham and Jim Wilson, Uncle Alec and the Grahams of Franz Josef. John McIndoe, 1983. p39
188. Graham & Wilson, p39.

Henry Newton

mountains. The Doctor was small of stature and slight, but extremely wiry, and he had a wonderful spirit. It was a sight to behold when he was travelling ahead of you with his swag on, carrying supplies to our base; he looked like a big bundle with two thin legs attached, and one wondered if they would stand the strain on the rough going. However, he always got there and generally had a little joke about the day's swagging when enjoying a mug of tea and a pipe after our arrival in camp.' So recollected Alec Graham.[189]

Newton had only been on the West Coast two months when Teichelmann invited him to go climbing in South Westland. Even for a clergyman, it was a baptism by fire. It took them ten days from their planned departure before Newton got his first view of the Franz Josef Glacier. They planned to leave on January 17, but it was so wet that their departure was delayed five days. Even then, on their first day they were held up by Evans Creek, near Harihari. Newton had a lot of trouble with his first river crossing. Later that day they reached the Wanganui River. The rain continued to fall like a depressing weight.[190]

> '... it was impossible to get the buggy across, so securing the swags with covers we took our cameras and boated across swimming the horses. At Hende's the accommodation house we were very glad of a warm West Coast fire and tea. All night the rain came down in torrents, and next day we could neither go on or back so we had to make the best of a "stick up" and pass the time with books and crib as best we could.'

189. Graham & Wilson, pp39, 40.
190. Newton diaries, Hocken Museum, 1902.

The following day they had to swim the horses across the Whataroa River and boat themselves and gear across. At The Forks Teichelmann rode on to Waiho, and Newton diverted to Okarito to conduct the first church service there in ten years.

Newton and Teichelmann asked Peter Graham to join them on the 1902 trip, but again he was unable to take leave from his employers. So on their arrival at Waiho (Franz Josef) the couple took along Mr Batson as a porter. He owned the guesthouse at Waiho. Even for those times, their equipment was rather sparse, and barely capable for the trip. There was only one ice axe between the three of them, which was Newton's. The Doctor had his prospecting pick. Batson, a man of the bush, had a slasher, but nothing in the way of alpine gear. Even his boots were considered inadequate. Teichelmann had a tent and a map, and Newton the rope. And of course there was the Doctor's camera. Teichelmann and Newton both had sleeping bags, but Batson only a blanket.

They tried a new route to Graham Saddle by initially following the miners' track up the Callery for a few kilometres. Bushman Batson then took them up the steep Callery Ridge, which is probably the one heading west from a confluence up towards Annie Peak. The consequence of this enterprising navigating was a night out in the bush with no water. They had to resort to squeezing moss for a brew. "It tasted a bit earthy but it quenched our thirst," remarked the Doctor.[191] It then took another whole day just to gain the main ridge and traverse along to the Waterhole above Rope Creek, a distance of about two kilometres.

Progress was better on the third day. They climbed up over Goatpath (1821m), past Thelma Peak (2087m) and onto the Salisbury Snowfield. From there it was a gentle climb to a saddle between St Mildred Peak and Newton Rocks, where they rested to scan the route. The snow was now soft from the sun, and plugging across the broad Geikie Snowfield tiring. Stops were frequent, and discussion went on. Eventually they reached the final steep climb up to Graham Saddle (2635m). Here, Newton was impressed with what Batson could achieve with his slasher, cutting useful sized steps up the slope.

It was late afternoon when they crossed Graham Saddle, the first from west to east. From here, they roped up for the descent of Rudolf Glacier. Teichelmann led, Batson

191. Graham & Wilson, p40.

The first crossing of Graham Saddle.
Aoraki Mt Cook in the Background.

was centre, and Newton with the best axe anchored the rear. This was fortunate, for just as they began the steep climb off the saddle, Batson slipped. Newton held his fall, but not without burning his fingers in the process. Batson was appropriately terrified, as the line of fall would have taken him all the way to the Tasman Glacier. Or so he would tell his listeners later. Nevertheless, it was a subdued party that continued slower and more cautiously.

They missed the turnoff to the de la Bêche bivouac rock, and ended up out on the Tasman Glacier. It was ten o'clock at night and they were worn out, so they camped there with nothing but a thin veneer of gravel between them and the ice. It was a cold night. Newton and Teichelmann were reasonably comfortable in their sleeping bags, but Batson shivered under his blanket.

"It's all very well for you fellows in sleeping bags, but I'm cold. I'm shivering."

Heartlessly the Doctor replied, "That's right, Batson, shiver as hard as you can, it's the natural way of getting warm."[192]

The following day, 1 February 1902, the trio reached Ball Hut at midday, overlooking

192. Peter Graham, op.cit. p51.

Ice tunnels on the Tasman Glacier

the Tasman Glacier. Jack Clarke and an Australian visitor arrived. Clarke, on approaching Teichelmann, Newton and Batson for the first time, and not yet having been introduced, couldn't decide which was the Rev. Newton. As Newton had grown quite a stubble and his hair frequently stood on end, Clarke looked them all over and decided the only reverend-looking gentleman was Batson. It was a story Batson enjoyed telling in later years.[193]

Next day a three and half hour walk took them to the Hermitage.

The trip was far from finished. Young Newton, fresh from a few seasons in the European Alps was keen to come back by a new route. At Ball Hut they had discussed possibilities with Jack Clarke. Clarke, who had made the first ascent of Mount Cook, was then Chief Guide at the Hermitage. He agreed to accompany them back to the West Coast from the Hooker Glacier via Baker Saddle.

Teichelmann and Newton felt a strong obligation to attempt the uncrossed Baker Saddle as 'we had promised Roberts to get some photos of the upper Strauchon'. But the exploratory spirit was equally strong. Newton wrote:

'So two plans were open to us, one to go over the Copland and take a day up the Strauchon or to go up the Hooker if we could get through the icefall and camp above it, thence over Baker Saddle, a new pass and down into the Copland that way.'[194]

Bad weather delayed them for two days during which they did a reconnaissance up the Hooker Glacier and spent one day playing 'bagatelle' at the Hermitage. Their first night was spent under overhanging rock on a rotten ridge below Baker Saddle. Stonefall was frequent, so shelter was most important. Batson had the bad luck to be the one sleeping on the outside. Once again it was a fitful night's sleep for him as rocks flew past perilously close. No doubt his imagination worked on him, as the smell of Hades and flashes of spark would add to his terror. Teichelmann, secure against the inside of the shelter, could only offer laconic advice and reassurances that did nothing for Batson.

Next day was a long climb up to the saddle, with some difficult pitches. Batson was in no state for appreciating the wonders of creation, but desperate to get off the tops.

---

193. Ibid, p51.
194. Newton diaries, 1902.

The Doctor was ahead of Batson on the rope, and had to frequently pull the trembling Batson up, terrified about those long exposed drops that seemed to beckon him down. "Let me get back to the bush; I feel safe there," he would plead to the Doctor.[195]

Jack Clarke, Dr. Parker, Rev. Newton and W. Batson at Ball Hut.

This was the first crossing of Baker Saddle (2192m). They climbed down through some awkward schrunds to the Strauchon Glacier and camped at the terminal face. From

195. Peter Graham, op.cit, p52.

there it was not far to the confluence with the Copland, just below Douglas Rock. Early the next morning while the others slept, the Doctor took several photos of Cook, Sefton and La Perouse, as well as the sleeping party among the boulders. Later while descending to the Copland River they struck thick bush and Teichelmann turned to Batson and said, "Here's your chance now, Batson, get into this with your billhook and whack away." Jack Clarke left them at the Copland River, returning to the Hermitage by Copland Pass. The remainder of the party traveled west, just crossing Architect Creek before it became impassable with the increasing rain. They camped in a hollow nearby, but had to resort to sitting under a tree at midnight, due to the water everywhere. Another miserable night for Batson.

Peter Graham step-cutting on the Franz Josef Glacier

Next day was trying. The food had long gone, and it took most of the day just to reach the Karangarua Flats. Sheep-catching efforts failed. After a few more kilometres and no sign of habitation, they gave up. But not Batson. He was desperate to get off this journey. He stumbled on, and met the two Mackintosh girls from the Scott homestead. They took him home, and sent horses back for the other two.

Teichelmann's concern for others and his wry sense of humour is further illustrated by his actions on arrival at the Scott's homestead. Batson had obviously pushed himself beyond his limits. Peter Graham takes up the story:

'Batson was well settled in bed

by that time, but the Doctor's first thought was for him, so they took a candle each and went in as if holding a wake. Very sunburnt with the skin peeling off his nose, and with a week's beard, he looked a picture. "Isn't he a beauty; and doesn't he look lovely there!" After a lot of raillery they left him to rest."[196]

This ended Teichelmann's 1902 trip. He later called in to see Peter and Alec Graham at Waiho and discussed their trip. The Doctor encouraged Peter and Alec to improve their climbing skills. On days off they would explore the Franz Josef Glacier using prospecting picks to cut steps. Soon they began taking local people for trips on the glacier and Teichelmann started referring people to get 'young Graham' to take them on the glacier.[197]

196. Ibid, p53.
197. Ibid, p53.

1903 Up the Fox Glacier to Pioneer Pass

In early 1903 Peter Graham received a letter from Dr Teichelmann informing him that he and Newton were organizing a trip to the head of Fox Glacier.[198] Graham was invited to join and accepted immediately. At that time the Fox névé was unexplored. Reverend Newton had assisted the Doctor in obtaining some clinker-nailed boots, as well as other alpine gear. He also found a local cobbler that could make a pair for Peter Graham, and a blacksmith to forge some crampons to suit the boots. There was no stopping this trio now.

Peter Graham arranged for all gear to be packed by horses over the bridle track from Waiho (Franz Josef) to Fox Glacier. As with many of their trips, their base camp was an old iron hut at the foot of the glacier. The first day was a reconnaissance only, taking swags several kilometres up the glacier past the first icefall. A few wet days followed, so Newton did some pastoral visitations. Teichelmann and Graham amused themselves by capturing a couple of pigeons, which they cooked with rice, onions, peas and suet dumplings. The Doctor was not a big eater, so Graham ate the larger share of one pigeon and the Doctor the rest. Newton arrived back later and cleaned up the whole of the other pigeon.

With some hard slog, the party put in a camp high up Chancellor Ridge. The next day they climbed to the top of the ridge and did the first ascent of Chancellor Dome (2004m). The view was stunning. Teichelmann and Newton set up their bulky plate cameras

198. Ibid, p63.

High Camp on the Chancellor Ridge

and photographed the virgin panorama before them. Newton was fascinated by the bulk of Horo Koau (Mount Tasman) and expressed a desire to attempt the arête from the col (later named Engineer Col) between Lendenfeld and Tasman.

They prepared for an exploratory trip to check out Newton's route. A platform of stones was built on the shoulder of a steep cliff facing the glacier, and the tent-fly erected over it. Later, fed and content, they lay chatting in their bags, the Doctor and Newton enjoying their evening smoke. Some stonefall disrupted the peace.

"That wall of yours, Peter, is it quite safe?" enquired the Doctor.

"Yes. No worries there," reassured Peter.

"That's good," replied Teichelmann. "You know I promised my wife I wouldn't go in any dangerous place."[199]

An early start saw them cross the névé to an impressively steep couloir rising from above a large schrund to the saddle between Tasman and Lendenfeld. Newton led, and Graham enlarged the steps, pleased with his skills. As Newton tired, his steps got smaller. At one point he tripped on his crampons, and fell head first. Graham held his fall, but the Doctor had stepped back to brace himself as well, and fell into a crevasse. Fortunately it was only to his waist. When they reached the col, the wind was quite strong, and very cold.

---

199. Ibid, p66.

Graham cut a hole in the cornice and lowered the Doctor through onto the eastern face. They all lunched there out of the wind, admiring the view. It was Peter's first look at the other side of the Divide. Were it not for the wind, they would have pressed on up onto Lendenfeld, but instead retreated to their lower camp.

Next day was a rest day, with Kea stew. Peter worried about how little the Doctor seemed to eat, and whether he would be capable of pulling his weight. Graham observed that Newton got short of breath easier, and blamed his smoking. He did revive easily from a rest, but Teichelmann was down for the day once he tired. When the Doctor admonished Newton for eating too much, he suggested that each carry his own food. That would lighten his load considerably, and increase the others. But he was not serious.

Pioneer Pass, Mt. Haast, Marcel Col, Lendenfeld and Engineer Col.

Teichelmann wanted to climb Pioneer Pass, the saddle north of Mount Haast. So back up to their bivvy they went, with sleeping bags, tent and food. After the glorious weather of the day before, the dawn brought ominous clouds out to sea. Taking the precaution of marking their route, they climbed towards the Divide via a narrow couloir between Mount Haast and Grey Peak. The wind was becoming stronger by the minute, and quite a lot of snow was in the air. On the pass, some swift consultation with Newton and he was persuaded by the others that to turn back was prudent. By now they had lost all visibility. They had to rest at their bivvy site, as both the Doctor and Graham suffered snowblindness. Newton had to lead Graham down the glacier the next day.

Back at the Chancellor Ridge campsite, they spent a few days, photographing and taking observations with a prismatic compass for chief surveyor, G. J. Roberts back in Hokitika. Peter Graham describes the careful attention Teichelmann gave his surveying.

> 'I erected a cairn with a firm flat stone on top on which to place the prismatic compass. The Doctor was very careful about taking three special points, Douglas Peak, Mount Haidinger, and Mount Tasman. I put down the number of the prismatic reading as he called it out. To make doubly sure that the readings were accurate, the Doctor took them again and was dismayed to find them all different. This was a poser until he realized the goggles he was wearing were affecting his compass needle. Afterwards he always removed them before taking any readings.'[200]

At the conclusion of the trip, Dr Teichelmann gave Peter Graham a rope, an ice-axe and a 'Badminton' book on mountaineering. Graham studied the book carefully and along with his younger brother Alec, worked on his skills. The Doctor's generosity and encouragement put Graham in a position to be able to guide Mr T. E. Donne, the first Superintendent of the Tourist Department, up the Franz Josef and Fox Glaciers in the winter of 1903. During the trip Donne said to Peter Graham, "Graham, you're just the type of man we're looking for. Would you go to The Hermitage as assistant to the Chief Guide, Jack Clarke, if I found you a position there?"[201]

Peter jumped at the opportunity.

This was the birth of the West Coast mountain guiding tradition that has continued unbroken to today. In October the same year Peter Graham crossed the Divide by the Copland Pass, to take up the position.[202]

---

200. Ibid, p65.
201. Ibid, p72.
202. Ibid, p75.

1904 First Crossing of Pioneer Pass

The summer of late 1903-early 1904 was exceptional for the amount of sunshine hours. Henry Newton noted that for a whole month there had been only one wet day. On top of that, the previous winter had been so miserly on snowfall that 'the hills seemed almost as clear as in the summer previous'.[203] Despite the dearth of snow, the annual expedition of 1904 by Newton and Teichelmann was taking shape. Teichelmann was keen to cross Pioneer Pass from the east, and had engaged Jack Clarke and Peter Graham as guides, while Newton and Alex Graham went up Fox Glacier. They planned to meet on the west. This was to complete the crossing partially undertaken from the west the previous year.

On the western side of the Alps, Alec Graham started some days ahead of Rev. Newton and with the help of Jack Sullivan of Weheka, swagged supplies up to Chancellor Ridge, to a site opposite Purgatory Creek. Jack and Alec enjoyed each others company and in the years to come, the Sullivan family of Weheka (later Fox) and the Graham family at Waiho (later Franz Josef) set up hotels at their respective locations and pioneered tourism at two of the world's most famous accessible glaciers.

Teichelmann left Hokitika by coach on 18 January, and arrived at The Hermitage in late January.[204] Always the explorer with a dash of surveyor and scientist, he investigated different glacier valleys and took a series of photographs of various peaks, acquainting

203. Newton Diaries, 1904.
204. Ibid.

himself better with the eastern side of the Divide. With Peter Graham he climbed up to the Sealy Range. From the top of Mount Ollivier (1933m), the Doctor, greatly impressed by the view, set up his full-plate camera and spent an hour taking photographs. The next day they set off for Ball Hut. At the meal table that night were a number of other visitors, including the Reverend Mr Hansell of Timaru, and two young Australian women. Peter Graham describes Teichelmann's conversation:

> 'In conversation... he made frequent references to the charm and outstanding beauty of the glacier, forest and lake scenery of Westland. We could hear, "We on the West Coast..." followed by a description of some of his climbing experiences or some beauty spot. Mr Hansell was very taken with the Doctor's enthusiasm for the West Coast and teasingly remarked to his table neighbour, "Let's see how long it will be before the Doctor mentions the West Coast again." He hadn't long to wait before the Doctor was in earnest conversation with the two Sydney girls, telling them of the attractions of Franz Josef Glacier. When opportunity offered, Mr Hansell with a mischievous twinkle asked the girls what they had in Sydney worth seeing.
>
> They replied with one voice, "We have a wonderful harbour."
>
> Hastily the Doctor rejoined, "Yes, yes, that's about all you have got."'[205]

Peter Graham and the Doctor walked up to Malte Brun Hut the next day, frequently photographing, and also scanning the route for the Pioneer Pass trip. Using the light to his advantage early the next morning, Teichelmann set up his camera at the end of the western arête of Malte Brun on a small rock platform, where he spent the morning photographing the overwhelming scenery before him. As usual, Peter had to keep a constant eye on the Doctor, even physically restraining him, as once he had his head under the black cloth of the camera, he was oblivious to the dangers around. Peter was quite relieved when the Doctor had finished and he could guide him to safer ground.[206]

At the beginning of February the Doctor set out again for Ball Hut with guides Jack Clarke and Peter Graham. They intended to cross Pioneer Pass between Mount Haast and Grey Peak. The party swagged up Haast Ridge with seven days' food and a large full

---

205. Peter Graham, op. cit. p87
206. Ibid, p88

Mt. Sefton and the Footstool. Stocking Glacier on the far right

plate camera and camped high on Haast Ridge at the levelled-off spot which had been used by earlier parties attempting to climb Mount Cook. It was rather exposed to the weather, especially from the north, so when a violent storm brought gale-force winds and heavy snow, they beat a hasty retreat to Ball Hut. Three days later they were back at the same camp site.

Henry Newton and Alex Graham were similarly affected by bad weather on the western side of the Divide.

It dawned fine on 7 February. Teichelmann and his party plodded up to Glacier

Dome in soft snow. Here they abandoned any thoughts of high climbing for the day and the morning was spent assisting Dr Teichelmann in taking photographs and checking out the route for the next day. While on the Dome, Peter Graham pointed out the col between Lendenfeld and Tasman he and the Doctor had reached the previous year. They had hardly finished explaining the climb when two distant figures appeared over the horizon from the western side of the Southern Alps. It could only be Reverend Newton and Alex Graham. The eastern party watched them move from Engineer Col slowly up Mount Lendenfeld in heavy, soft snow, before they eventually turned back.

Camp on Haast ridge

Jack Clarke said he wanted to cooee and shout out to them, but Dr Teichelmann quickly replied, "No, no, don't do that. If Newton heard you he would want to climb straight down to us." Teichelmann knew well the impetuosity of youth and advised New Zealand's most experienced guide against such a course of action. At the same time he was shaping the future of two of the country's upcoming guides, the Graham brothers. He was quite concerned about Alex Graham, as he was still very inexperienced, and did not have particularly good equipment. The party watched Newton and Alex Graham disappear out of sight, presumably back to the Fox névé.[207]

The next morning, Dr Teichelmann and his guides retraced their footsteps up to Glacier Dome and followed the prominent arête leading up to Mount Haast. The Doctor climbed easily up the broken rock to where a band of red slate slashes the ridge. From there they traversed for a long way, out over a steep snow slope, until they were in the basin under the eastern side of Mount Dixon. This traverse entailed considerable risk, as it was a slope frequently strafed by rockfall, some boulders leaving vertical wounds in the snow a metre deep. Jack Clarke led out in waist deep snow to the pass, stopping only to negotiate the final schrund. Its softness defied their first attempts, and they had to resort to some combined tactics: standing on the Doctor's shoulders. It was a relief to reach the pass. The views were impressive to both sides. They trudged down the West Coast side of the Divide, pleased to find Newton and Alex Graham's footsteps of the previous day to guide them through the labyrinth of crevasses.

The dry winter and warm summer had created particularly large and numerous slots, and the tracks of Newton and Graham saved them considerable time.

When they came to the Newton/Graham high camp, they left some biscuits and dates there for the next climb, to save carrying them back up in the morning. Then it was off down to base camp.

Alex Graham had been hoping to meet Jack Clarke for some time. 'I was especially looking forward to meeting Jack Clarke, whom I had heard so much about as a mountaineer

---

207. Peter Graham, op cit., Alec Graham and Jim Wilson, op cit., and Newton diaries.

and guide. I think I regarded Jack with something amounting to hero worship for his prowess and for the fact that he was one of the party to first conquer Mount Cook.'[208]

Jack Sullivan and Peter Graham near the snout of the Fox Glacier

That afternoon Alex Graham met his hero on Chancellor Ridge when Clarke arrived with Teichelmann and Peter Graham. There was much excitement and conversation. History was made that day. The first crossing of Pioneer Pass was posted and more importantly, plans were cemented for the future, a future in which these five climbers were going to play a leading role in New Zealand mountaineering for decades to come.

The next morning was overcast, so Newton and Alex Graham descended from their high camp to base camp to make plans for the next day with the others. The Graham brothers baked several large loaves of damper. The Doctor thought that they would now have sufficient food for a climb, as there was the stash at the high camp. Newton's face dropped. Being a honest chap, he revealed much in his facial expressions. It was the Reverend's turn for confession: he and Alex had scoffed the lot during the night!

Two days later the group decided to head for the unclimbed Glacier Peak and Mount Douglas. They climbed up to Pioneer Ridge and discovered a patch of gravel at the top of a steep buttress and noted it as a future tent or hut site. But time ran out, and they descended the Fox Glacier back to Weheka (Fox) and then on to Waiho.

---

208. Alec Graham and Jim Wilson, op cit., p43.

Jack Clarke had been suffering terribly from toothache during the trip, so on 13 February, Dr Teichelmann took him to Okarito, where two teeth and three stumps were extracted. Jack Heveldt, the proprietor of the Forks Hotel, had been given a pair of forceps, along with a rudimentary book on dental extraction that had formerly belonged to Dick Dickens of Okarito. After the bush dentistry, Jack Clarke returned to the Hermitage with Peter Graham by way of Goat Path and Graham Saddle.[209]

Teichelmann returned to medical duties in Hokitika where much of his work was surgical. One of the Doctor's fears was damaging his hands when climbing for this would affect his ability to perform delicate operations. Before climbing on rock his fingers would be taped to prevent cuts and abrasions. Alex Graham wrote that 'he was always worried about letting his wife down, and being hurt or even dying from a fall.'[210]

---

209. Peter Graham, op. cit., p90. Newton diaries. Graham & Wilson, p46.
210. Graham & Wilson, op cit.

1905 Harper Saddle and Mount Cook

Visits from Rev. Newton and Dr Teichelmann to Waiho, and the next trip into the mountains, were what Alec Graham lived for in his formative days as a fledgling mountain guide. Some months after the 1904 expedition, the Rev. Newton visited Waiho on one of his regular parish visits. After the church service the two got together and pored over photographs of the trip, re-living the special moments and achievements once more.

For their 1905 expedition, Teichelmann and Newton chose the Cook River. This is a deeply glaciated river valley that has a fearsome reputation. The upper Cook River receives water from La Perouse Glacier, the Balfour Glacier and Gulch Glacier. Even today, this valley would have only one or two parties every decade visiting its nearly impenetratable bush and gorges.

Charlie Douglas and Arthur P Harper had reached the terminal face of La Perouse Glacier in 1894, but the upper reaches were little known.

Ten days before Newton arrived, Alec Graham and Arthur Woodham started cutting a track and packing gear up the valley. They took horses as far as Diggers' huts, about a mile upstream from the present bridge. After spending a number of wet days packing up the valley, the pair established a base camp about two miles above Tony's Rock and then returned to meet the others.

On Monday January 16 1905, Rev Newton left Scott's house 'after a week of services among the scattered settlers' and headed for the Miners' Hut with Alex Graham, where he had arranged to meet Teichelmann. Unfortunately Teichelmann hadn't arrived, so next morning Newton and Graham packed up to Castle Rock, a few miles beyond the junction of the Balfour River. Graham waited here for Doctor Teichelmann while Newton tramped up to Tony's Rock. This enormous erratic boulder is 100 feet high and is 700 feet around three sides of the base. Woodham arrived that afternoon with another load. For the next two days Graham and Newton slashed a track up the valley. Six days after Newton arrived at Tony's Rock, Dr Teichelmann finally appeared having been delayed by floods.

The Cook River Valley

Newton writing in the Alpine Club Journal explained the difficulty thus far: "It had taken two men, working continuously for a fortnight, to get the base camp in, a matter of nine miles, a distance equal to that of Evolena from the Rhone Valley, though not so great a rise."[211]

211. Newton Dairies

Newton, Teichelmann and Alec Graham left Arthur Woodham at the base camp to do some gold-prospecting while they pushed on up to the snout of La Perouse Glacier, which was then a further two miles up the valley. Here they found a spot for a high camp at the end of the north spur of La Perouse.

After a spell of bad weather and a brief excursion up the La Perouse Glacier to check the route towards Harper Saddle, the party left at 2.30am on 29 January 1905.[212] At first light they were at the foot of a crumbling rock ridge, heading for the pass. Nearing the top, they struck a difficult pitch, where Newton took a tumble, but fortunately the impact of the fall was cushioned by his swag full of sleeping bags. Alec Graham was a little bemused by Teichelmann's reaction.

The Little Doctor was funny over this for as he went to help Mr Newton, he whispered to me "I warned you, Alec, that Newton was impetuous sometimes."[213]

They reached Harper Saddle about 3:00am, descended to Hooker Glacier and camped at the present day site of Gardiner Hut. It was getting towards the end of Newton's holiday and he felt the need to get back to take church services the following Sunday. Neither wanted to go back by the same route so it appears Teichelmann talked Newton into going up to the bivouac on Haast Ridge with the view of crossing the saddle between Silberhorn and Malispina (now called Clarke Saddle) and then back to their camp in the Cook River below La Perouse Glacier. Well pleased with the first crossing of Harpers Saddle, the party left next morning for The Hermitage to be warmly welcomed by the McDonald family. Waiting for Dr Teichelmann was Scottish climber, R.S. Low, who was hoping the Doctor would join him on a planned ascent of Mount Cook by Zurbriggen's route. Jim Wilson, author of Aorangi, writes that Newton should have smelt a rat at this, but protests he went up in all innocence in an attempt to get back to his waiting parishioners.[214]

Writing in the 1915 for the English Alpine Club Journal, Newton says: I am still convinced that Teichelmann and the others had put this up behind my back, and I am still doubtful about the great difficulties in connection with the pass.

---

212. Ibid
213. Alec Graham & Jim Wilson, op.cit
214. Jim Wilson, Aorangi

Alec Graham, Henry Newton and Dr. Teichelmann after the first crossing of Harper Saddle

After a welcome bath and an excellent meal at The Hermitage, Teichelmann and Newton were beginning to feel a lot of pain from snowblindness which Newton described as being from "the wood smoke of the camp and then the fog on the pass, which had compelled us to take off our glasses, had irritated them considerably.

Newton goes on to describe a practice which could land someone in jail today. "We found some cocaine in the hotel, and by injecting that and using a tea leaf compress we were able to get some sleep."[215]

215. Newton Diaries

Dr Teichelmann always made a point after these trips into the mountains, of telegraphing his wife of his safe arrival, so next morning while Alec Graham rode to Glentanner Station to send some telegrams, Guides Jack Clarke and Peter Graham left with the remaining three climbers for Ball Hut.[216]

The party at Haast Ridge bivvy.

The next day, 3 February 1905, the group camped at the bivouac site on the Haast Ridge, and went up to Glacier Dome for a look at the route to Clarke Saddle.

---

216. Alec Graham and Jim Wilson, op.cit.

Aoraki Mount Cook taken from near Glacier Dome.

"Here Teichelmann proceeded to do some fast talking. His enthusiasm was aroused at the thought of an ascent of Cook, rearing so magnificently across the Plateau. He hated the thought of slipping back to the Coast without attempting such a climb. On the other hand he could hardly desert Newton. He enlisted the help of the guides, and Newton was gravely told that the saddle he wished to cross was very difficult, that it would take too long to cross into the La Perouse. Newton suspected it was a put-up job but, he writes, "there was nothing for it but to submit to their plan." So tame a submission suggests that the call of his Sunday services were all but drowned out by the music of Cook's shining ridges."[217]

The next morning at 4:00am, they set off to reconnoitre the route for the following day. On reaching Glacier Dome they descended to the Grand Plateau and walked to the foot of Zurbriggen's route, and climbed up the steep 3000 foot route, with Clarke and Graham alternating with the step cutting. What had started out as a reconnaissance was turning out to be the final climb. On the summit rocks they found a tin matchbox Green and his guide Kaufmann had left twenty-three years before. At the start of the ice cap, Jack Clarke turned to the group and said, "Now we shall have to consider whether we should go on or turn back - if we go on, there is every chance of our having to spend the night out, which is not advisable; if we turn back we shall no doubt be able to get off the mountain before darkness."

The Doctor said, "Well, Clarke, we will leave that to you.'

Jack said, "I don't think that is quite fair."

However, the Doctor repeated, "No, we will leave it to you Clarke. You are the leader."[218]

Clarke didn't hesitate, and instead of answering, headed up the ridge to the summit.

Throughout the eight years since arriving in Hokitika, on fine days Dr Teichelmann had woken up to superb views of Aoraki Mount Cook from his home in Hampden

---

217. Jim Wilson, op.cit.
218. Ibid.

Street. On his medical forays to South Westland, he would see it from virtually every known viewpoint. He wanted to get to the top. So when Clarke headed upwards towards the summit, he cheered spontaneously together with Newton, Low and Peter Graham. None of them had really wanted to turn back and were now prepared to throw caution to the wind.

The successful party after the 3rd ascent of Mt. Cook.
Teichelmann sitting on right.

Within 100 feet from the top, Clarke let Graham cut the final steps to the summit. This was the third ascent of Mount Cook. Peter Graham recalls the moment:

"Everybody was delighted at gaining the summit. The Little Doctor was enormously pleased for my sake and told many of his friends, 'I believe, Peter, you know, led to the summit.' He was always most generous with his praise and made me feel as though he regarded me as his special protégé."[219]

With evening coming on they had little time to admire the view from the top. The vista was magnificent - almost beyond description, recalls Peter Graham. Mount Cook chronicler, Jim Wilson, refers to the friendly interaction that was a feature of the relationship between Teichelmann and Newton:

219. Peter Graham, Mountain Guide

"Then they began the long descent. A vivid sunset bathed the surrounding peaks in pink light as they climbed down the summit rocks, and the enthusiastic Teichelmann quite forgot the seriousness of their situation as he excitedly exclaimed over the beautiful sight. There was always genial byplay going on between Teichelmann and Newton, and on this occasion, as Graham recalls, the vicar had gently to admonish the Doctor: "Now, now, Doctor, we haven't time to stop and admire everything; it's getting late, we must get down."[220]

At 9:00pm they reached their packs which had been left on a rocky outcrop just above the junction of Zurbriggen's Ridge and Bowie Ridge. Here they spent a sleepless night huddled together, and the next morning at the bottom of the ridge met a very relieved Alec Graham who had come to meet them. They headed down to Ball Hut and then out to The Hermitage.

Now the climb was over, Newton once more become concerned about his parishioners' well being and planned a quick dash over Copland Pass. A sudden storm prevented this and Newton was resigned to missing out on yet another Sunday's sermon. When the weather cleared, Alec Graham, Teichelnann and Newton returned to the West Coast via Copland Pass.

220. Jim Wilson, op.cit.

1906 Cook River and Mount La Perouse

Flushed with the success of their 1905 expedition, the West Coast trio decided on the Cook River again, and the unclimbed Mount La Perouse as their main objective. They were joined this time by their companion from the Mount Cook climb: the Scottish climber, Mr R. S. Low. Greatly liked by the Doctor and the Reverend for his good natured humour and quiet, unassuming manner, Low was regarded as a skilled climber on both rock and snow. Another prospector, Charles Anderson, helped Alec Graham set up a base camp, a little higher than last year's one. Anderson had been working a gold claim in the Cook River, opposite the Digger's Huts. He was a true bushman, sleeping in one blanket and a cocoon of ferns. Alec Graham was amused at the sight of smoke seeping out of a pile of ferns as he settled down for the night with his final pipe, rather like a talking haangi (a Maori cooking pit).

When Newton arrived at Waiho on 17 January, he was pleasantly surprised to be reunited with an ice axe he had lost four years earlier on his first trip to the glacier. It had been discovered just a few days previous to his arrival, with its shaft sticking out of the ice of the glacier terminus. Apart from rust on the pick, it was in good order. Teichelmann, Low and Newton joined up with Alec Graham about a week later, and they swagged up the Cook River to La Perouse Glacier. A high camp was made on the spur which separates Gulch Creek and La Perouse Glacier. They had good views of the head of the valley, plenty of firewood, and a stream nearby. They even had sugar and biscuits from the year before.

It dawned fine on 1 February, 1906, but with fog in the valley below. The party of

La Perouse Glacier and Mt. La Perouse (partially obscured by cloud)

four left the high camp just before 4:00am and soon crested the main ridge. They had to traverse around two steep dips on the ridge before reaching the col and ridge leading up to the summit of La Perouse. It took a whole hour to negotiate the first gendarme. They had attacked it head on, only to discover that there was no way down off the other side. So back they went. Newton was last to descend, and his camera once again caused him grief. Determined to avoid the problems of 1905, he tied it to his rope and lowered it off. It kept snagging on rock projections, and it suffered damage with the crashing about. Later he was dismayed to find the shutter damaged. A rest day with the equivalent of a Swiss army knife and he had manufactured new parts sufficient for its continued use during that expedition.

The climb was straightforward, although a fair number of steps were required. They were pleased to find that the arête that had looked so sharp and steep from the Cook River flats was not too bad in reality. It was in excellent condition with a good firm coating of snow. It was a thrill for Alec Graham, who recalled his feelings of that moment. 'It was my first real mountain, and a 10,000 foot virgin peak.'[221]

It was only 10.50am when they stepped the final rise. There was plenty of time to linger on the top and take in the stunning view, especially of neighbouring Mount Cook, and to relive the excitement of the previous year. Newton carefully studied an unclimbed route on Mount Cook, known today as Earle's route. He expressed his desire to return one day to climb it.[222] And as they sat on the summit, one wonders if they thought themselves a weird bunch. A Scot, an Englishman, a German/Scot born in Australia, and a New Zealander sitting on a peak named after a French navigator. Teichelmann, Newton and Alec Graham had forged not only friendships, but had become a formidable climbing combination that was on the brink of greatness.

They descended by a different route, using a snow slope on the La Perouse Glacier side. This was the route later used in 1948 by the famous Ruth Adams rescue party, which included Sir Edmund Hillary. Using judicious glissading, they returned to camp in just one hour 27 minutes, compared with over six hours for the ascent.

A few days of bad weather followed and the group explored the La Perouse Glacier. From it they climbed up to a col on the Balfour Range, which lies opposite Katies Col on the Fox Range. They had a good view of the upper Balfour Glacier and its spectacular display of avalanches from the hanging section down onto the lower glacier. Clarke Saddle was identified further east: another objective. To the south they traced their route over Harper Saddle. Just to the east of that sat the imposing bulk of Mount Hicks, then known by the more lyrical name of St David's Dome. As it was also an objective, they carefully scoped out routes from the north, and even a potential bivvy site. That done, they got up and traversed east to climb a small rock peak. It is unclear whether this was Vanguard or a closer rock pinnacle.

Dr Teichelmann's much traveled full plate camera was carried to this spot. Alec Graham, who spent much of his early guiding years carrying the Doctor's camera best describes his passion.

221. Alec Graham & Jim Wilson op. cit.
222. Ibid, p57.

Dampier, Cook and St. David's Dome (Mt. Hicks)
From Balfour Range

'The Doctor was very thorough in everything he undertook and it took a long time, sometimes, to get just the right composition he wanted. He never failed to ask me to look through the viewfinder to see if I could suggest any improvement, for he always liked me to help him. When on any sharp peak I put the rope on him as he was so interested in getting what he wanted that he was liable to forget where he was standing when he had his head under the focusing cloth. Then, when he was satisfied with the composition of the picture he was taking, there was the right aperture and time for the exposure to be carefully adjusted and checked.

Mr Newton would sometimes get a little impatient with the Doctor for taking so long. The Doctor would reply, "I'm not going to let Alec carry the camera all the way up here and then make a mess of it. The difference between you and me, Newton, is that is that you are a photographic climber and I am a climbing photographer!" '[223]

Next morning they set off for Clarke Saddle, but heavy snow and deteriorating

223. Ibid, pp58 & 59

weather at the second icefall repulsed them. The next day the elements kept them at bay, enforcing time for repairs and ablutions, philosophizing and observing.

David's Dome (Hicks) and Mt. Cook from Opul Glacier below Harper's Saddle

The four explorers had waged some competition with the wekas and keas over ownership of certain items. For some unknown reason, their soap was in particular demand from the wekas (New Zealand native bird). When the Doctor decided to wash a shirt the following wet day, there was only one small piece remaining. The other three sat and watched as one particular weka stalked through the scrub towards where the Doctor sat washing by the stream. Bemused, they kept silent. Every time he put the soap down on a rock, the weka would line up an attack, to be foiled at the last minute by the unsuspecting Doctor picking it up again. Finally, the weka struck in a lightning raid, and raced off into the scrub with the enraged Doctor in pursuit. The soap was lost, but the audience deemed the entertainment well worth the price.

When the weather cleared at their base camp on the La Perouse Glacier, they readied themselves for the next objective: St. David's Dome, now called Mount Hicks. Unfortunately the Doctor had bruised his heel and elected not to join. It was late in the afternoon when Newton, Low and Alec Graham left for a higher bivouac below the first ice fall on the La Perouse Glacier. That night as they ate their meal, Newton remarked how he missed the Doctor's company, but said it was rather nice having a meal without the Doctor's eye on you. Graham and Newton had wolf-like appetites, while the Doctor, a small eater, would jokingly remark that it was no wonder they had to carry such heavy swags.

On 9 February the party got away at 2:30am on a very warm morning. Following their previous route through the first icefall, they turned right on to a long snow ridge running down from Mount. Hicks (referred to in Anderson's Jubilee History of South Canterbury as the north-west arête), joined the main west ridge higher up. They struck soft snow on the lower part of the ridge, but step cutting became necessary higher up where conditions were colder. At the top of the north-west ridge, they struck a rock face which provided excellent climbing onto the main west ridge. The final section of ridge to the summit was climbed in gusty conditions. The force of the wind necessitated a straddle shuffle along one section of the icy ridge. They reached the top at 11:00am. It was so windy there that Newton had to lie down to take his photographs. Sheltering from the wind on the eastern lee of the summit, they had time to admire the neighbouring flanks of Cook and Dampier.

The descent was by the same route. It had been a long time since they had last quenched their thirst, so a stop was made on the rocks just before the glacier. The billy packed ready with snow, Newton got out the bottle of meths. In a second, it had slipped from his hand and shattered on the rocks. The meths quickly evaporated. Without a word, but with parched mouths worsened by anticipation, they packed up and continued on.

Meanwhile, back at base camp, Dr Teichelmann was having an enjoyable day with his camera. His heel injury was rapidly improving. He was obviously pleased with the first ascent of Mount Hicks by his team mates and congratulated them warmly and enthusiastically on their return. They were more interested in the contents of the boiling billy than his congratulatory speech.

Mr Newton and Dr Teichelmann were running out of holiday time, so they returned to their respective employments in Ross and Hokitika.[224] Their companion Mr Low, whom they had come to respect and like, travelled back with them as far as Waiho. Alec Graham and Charlie Stoner transported out the remainder of their gear.

R.S. Low's route was across the snow shelf top left and Franz Josef neve to Graham Saddle. (top right) Alec Graham left Low here to travel alove down the normally safe route to the de la Beche Bivvy rock

224. Ibid, p61.

When Alec Graham returned to his home in Waiho, Mr Low was there and somewhat anxious to return to The Hermitage via Graham Saddle. He asked Graham to accompany him part of the way. The next day they camped under a rock on the Baird Range, below Goat Path.

> 'We started early next morning and I went with him well out over the Franz Josef snowfields. Here we parted and I returned to the base of Mildred Peak and watched him cross the saddle. I did not feel anxious about him going alone, for he was a very careful and safe climber and should have reached Ball Hut before I got back home.'[225]

It was 10:00am, Wednesday 21 February, when Alex Graham headed home to Waiho from near the Mackay Rocks. An hour later Mr Low was ready to descend into the Rudolf Glacier, having safely crossed Graham Saddle. He stopped for a short rest at the top of a couloir that led down onto the glacier. Conditions were good, and progress swift, so he resolved to travel right through to the Hermitage that day, rather than spend a night at Ball Hut. He bent and picked up his swag. It was bulky, but not heavy. He had only brought provisions for one day in order to travel light and fast. Shouldering his swag, and picking up his ice axe, he stepped carefully down into the couloir.

Not bothering to cut steps, he slipped into the repetitive rhythm of placing the axe firmly, then stepping down. Thoughts elsewhere, he was caught unawares when his feet slipped on a small patch of ice. Quickly he rolled into a self-arrest position to brake his accelerating fall. Panicking, he drove the axe in hard. His momentum was too great, and the axe was wrenched from his hands. By now he had gathered considerable speed, and a hungry schrund below opened wide in expectation. It was not to be. Slamming into some protruding rocks, he heard and felt his ankle crunch and twist. The pain was excruciating, and he knew it was unusable. If not broken, it was at least badly dislocated.

Low dragged himself to safety behind some big rocks and collapsed. Wisely, he rested there. His racing thoughts gradually slowed, and he formulated a plan. He was a long way from anyone, and would not be missed for some time. He may be crippled, but one look at the gaping schrund below at the base of the couloir, and he realized that those

---

225. Ibid, pp61, 62.

rocks had undoubtedly saved his life. He had lost his ice axe and all his food, except for a tin of milk and some chocolate. At least he had plenty of tobacco, he thought, lighting his pipe. The options were grim. To descend meant a crawl with no ice axe down a hard frozen slope. Waiting for the sun, he needed the softened surface to gain some friction on the slope. Carefully, with two hands and one boot, he inched down to a snowbridge over the crevasse. An icy breath from the depths of the blue/black maw sent a shiver down his spine as he crawled across to the safety of the glacier. Now seated, he propelled himself out onto the centre of the glacier. There he spent the night, thankful for the insulation of his sleeping bag.

It took three painful days in snow and cold to crawl down the glacier, dragging himself along the last day in two feet of fresh hail and snow. Waiting for the assistance and comfort of the sun, he leashed his pack to one end of his rope, and himself to the other. Dragging himself a rope length, he would then wind in his pack. In this manner he passed his second day. That night was spent sheltered behind a large rock on the ice. His fierce thirst could be slaked with small pools of meltwater, or dribbles on rocks. Once he had gained the moraine, he had to crawl with his pack on. Its bulk exaggerated his movements, and balance was awkward. It snowed heavily that night. The de la Bêche rock bivouac was only three kilometres away, but it took all day, crawling over rough moraine and through sixty centimetres of snow to get there.

For another six days Low waited, living on a hundred grams of cocoa found in the bivvy, half a loaf of bread he had recently found in the bottom of his swag, and water collected from drips on the rock. As the days passed and his meagre supplies diminished, so did his hopes of ever being rescued. He wrote his last requests on the mica sheets of a headlamp, and with his own blood he wrote his thanks to his climbing friends on a map that Alec Graham had lent him.

Four days after Alec Graham had seen Mr Low go over Graham Saddle, he and Dr Teichelmann were worried by the non-arrival of telegrams which Low promised he would send when he arrived safely at the Hermitage. Both Alec and the Doctor wired the telephonist at Tekapo, who sent a message by pigeon to the Hermitage. Foolishly, the telegrapher tied the whole telegram to the pigeon's leg who, after having pecked it off, flew to The Hermitage without it.

The de la Beche Bivvy rock where R.S. Low spent over a week

Nine days after his accident, two friends of Low arrived in Waiho, having crossed the Copland from the Hermitage. One was Professor Marshall, and the other Doctor Bell. Low was engaged to be married to Dr Bell's sister. They had been waiting at the Hermitage for Low to join them, so when they heard that he had left nine days before, they were justifiably concerned. The nearest telephone was 15 kilometres north at the Forks, but eventually a message was passed to Lake Pukaki, the closest telephone to the Hermitage. Realizing the importance of the eaten telegram, someone rode at speed through to the Hermitage. Jack Clarke and Peter Graham set off at once, even though it was 8:00pm. Fearing the worst, they traveled through the night, knowing that it would be at least de la Bêche corner before they would find any sign of him. At 4:00am they were relieved to hear Low's answers to their calls as they climbed up from the Tasman Glacier.[226]

226. Ibid, p62.

'Though terribly thin, Mr Low was able to sit up and tell us what happened. His first request was for tobacco, which Jack was able to supply. He was very hungry so I made some soup and gave him small but frequent helpings while Jack examined his injuries. There were abrasions on his face and hands and a fractured ankle, but he was suffering most pain from his knees. They were severely lacerated after crawling two miles over broken moraine.'[227]

The best Peter Graham could do in the way of a mountain radio was to carry on his back the carrier pigeon, Dick Seddon, named after another famous West Coaster. Battered and ruffled, he was entrusted with requesting a doctor and others to come and help. Twenty minutes after repairs in the sun on a rock, Dick was back at the Hermitage.[228] Later that day, with great relief, Dr Teichelmann received word in Hokitika that his friend was alive.

Peter and Jack then raced over Graham Saddle to the Waterhole below Goatpath, where they met Newton and reported the good news of the discovery. Later the following day they were back with Low, to assist the nine men who had arrived to transport Low. The doctor who had joined them was Dr Truby King of Plunket fame.

It took ten hours to carry Low to Ball Hut. There they strapped him to a mattress on Hanmer Jack, an old grey horse, renown for his sure footing. He was met by a coach that took him through to Timaru for x-rays. Transferred to Christchurch, Low then suffered further complications which nearly cost him his life. Eventually he recovered, and went on to do some more climbing, but it was never the same again due to the chronic ankle injury.

Low's dramatic rescue brought mountaineering to the front pages of all New Zealand newspapers. Up to this time, it was Malcolm Ross who brought mountaineering to the attention of the public using a style that John Pascoe regarded derisively: 'He was too wedded to his easy-come-easy-go journalism and his uncritical gusto got the better of him.'[229] But regardless of style, Ross popularised mountaineering. Teichelmann also

---

227. Peter Graham, p122.
228. Ibid.
229. John Pascoe, Land Uplifted High. Whitcombe and Tombes, p204.

contributed greatly to popular literature of New Zealand mountaineering before the First World War with entertaining articles superbly illustrated with photographs in various magazine and newspaper supplements.

Not long after Mr. Low's miraculous rescue, the Doctor received word from Australia that his mother, Margaret Teichelmann, had died on 30 March 1906 at the age of 82.

1907 First ascent galore - Head of the Fox Glacier

Mr Newton's time in New Zealand was drawing to a close, and 1907 would see the last of the five annual expeditions that Newton, Teichelmann and Alec Graham undertook as a team. This time, Newton had a much longer holiday period at his disposal, six weeks, and he persuaded the Doctor to go with him up the Fox Glacier. They had long fancied the idea of putting a camp on Pioneer Ridge and using it as a base for climbing many accessible peaks flanking the névé.

The fine weather in late December 1906 and early January 1907 augured well for a fine summer. The West Coast Times announced on 9 January, "The long hot summer continues, with the Fire Brigade having to fill householders' empty water tanks." It had been continuous wet weather right up until Christmas, but had been brilliant ever since then.

As was usual, food and equipment were dispatched south by ship, this time on the *Jane Douglas* a couple of months before the trip started. Mr Newton and Dr Teichelmann hired Herman Osmers from Ross to go south and help Alec Graham pack food up the Fox Glacier. Herman Osmers biked from Ross to Waiho on 7 January, 1907.[230] (It is interesting to note that Herman Osmers' great-grandson Ted Brennan lives in Ross, and is an active tramper and climber.)

Today climbers can drive from Hokitika to Franz Josef in an hour and a half, and

230. Alec Graham & Jim Wilson, op.cit.

from there get a helicopter to Pioneer Hut, all within two hours of leaving Hokitika. It took Herman Osmers and Alec Graham (with the later arrival of Teichelmann and Newton) fourteen days until they were established in a high camp on Pioneer Ridge, ready for the first climb. This entailed a number of packing trips up Fox Glacier.

While food was dispatched by ship, the climbers had to travel by horse and coach

With Newton and Alec Graham being young, fit men, Teichelmann tried to keep his fitness level up by cycling and walking when possible, but with such a busy schedule, he didn't always find time. To get his calf muscles, back and shoulders in shape, he struck upon a way to get climbing fit. He would put a large ladder up the side of his house, and with a moderately heavy back pack on, he would climb up and down the ladder for as long as he could manage.

Initially this was a source of great amusement for his neighbours in Hampden Street. In 1990, this old ladder was still on the property.[231] Alec Graham frequently told this story to friends when the subject of fitness came up, recalls Dorothy Fletcher.

The party were well settled in their high camp at the foot of Pioneer Ridge by 20 January, ready to start the climbing programme. As both Teichelmann and Newton were a little out of form, despite the fact that Newton had been carrying swags for five days, they elected to climb with their cameras up what they called the Buttress, which is part of Pioneer Ridge.[232] From the top of the buttress they got some excellent panoramas of the Alps and névés. Herman Osmers left the party at this stage and returned to Ross. A few

231. Denis Pfahlert, ex-Fox mountain guide. Personal Conversation, 1991
232. Newton Diaries, 1907

days of bad weather followed, and some trips were undertaken to lower camps before they were ready for the first climb to Mount Halcombe.

The reason for climbing Mount Halcombe was due to its location on the range between the Fox and Franz névé, and for the view it afforded to Glacier Peak and Mount Douglas. They left shortly after 5:00am on 26 January, and headed for the saddle on the western side of Mount Halcombe. They had difficulty getting across a large bergschrund, and after a long stint of step cutting finally reached the saddle. With the heavy full-plate camera, and Newton's lighter Sandison camera, the party of three carried over twenty-five kilograms of camera gear. This slowed them down on the climb to the top, which they reached later that morning. From the summit the Doctor was bubbling with excitement as he set up the full-plate camera. The routes up Glacier Peak and Mount Douglas were carefully studied. By 2:00 pm they were back at the camp preparing for another climb. That evening as they curled up in their sleeping bags and watched the darkness descend, Dr Teichelmann, moved by the beauty around him, quoted these lines from Longfellow:

"The day is done and the darkness
Falls from the wings of night
Like a feather is wafted downwards
From an eagle in its flight."[233]

The billy was boiling shortly after 2:00am and they set out at 4:00am, reaching the foot of Glacier Peak by 5:30am. The route up Glacier Peak was initially close in to the rock spur running down from the north shoulder. The first schrund was crossed without difficulty, and then they stopped in a hole out of the wind for a second breakfast. At 6:15am they set off again. The second schrund posed some trouble - Newton had to borrow a second ice axe and some assistance from Alec to gain the upper lip, then passed the tool down to Teichelmann for his ascent. Steps were cut up the steep slope to the final schrund in a line to the summit. Sastrugi had to be continually chopped away on the summit slopes, as the rope kept catching annoyingly around them. At 7:55am they had reached the end of the climb.[234] They were all quite surprised at the ease with which they climbed Glacier Peak, for it had a fearsome reputation from the east. Again using Newton's

233. Henry Wadsworth Longfellow, 'The Day is Done'. Stanza one.
234. Newton Diaries, 27 January 1907.

camera, they took numerous summit shots. The view down onto the Rudolf Glacier revealed just how far Low had crawled after his solo accident. Westwards they could see right down to Cone Rock near the terminus of the Fox Glacier. Beside them, Douglas Peak looked as impossible as ever from where they stood, but it was agreed they would attempt it the following day.

Mount Douglas - Newton regarded Mt. Douglas as the finest climb in New Zealand

Away at 4:30am the next morning, they followed their tracks up past Glacier Peak, and were soon on the slopes of Mount Douglas. Two gendarmes, visible from Mount Halcombe, presented an awesome aspect. The first was successfully traversed, and the second had a cleft through its centre, providing passage for the climbers. They halted at 10:15am for an early lunch, and to scan the route and discuss tactics. There were further difficulties along the final ridge to the summit, with a very steep rock face that appeared to offer no routes at all. Some chimneys on the western face provided some sound rock, positive climbing, and hope for a successful summit. After a short rest below the snow arête, Newton cut and stamped steps to the summit. But another appeared 40 metres away. Silently, the Reverend led on, too lazy to cut steps, and shuffled along the cheval ridge with one leg either side. The top was reached at 1:45pm Some chocolate and figs found in pockets had to suffice for the celebratory meal.

This was a brilliant first ascent of a mountain which up until then had been regarded as being very difficult - if not impossible. It has an imposing presence when viewed from the Fox névé. It was their third first ascent in as many days, and one of their most satisfying.

Newton regarded Mount Douglas as his finest climb in New Zealand, and Alec Graham wrote, 'To me, it still takes first place'. [235]

Alec Graham and Rev Newton just below the summit of Mt. Torres.

The descent was long and slow. It took until 5:00pm to reach their food, left in the care of the gendarmes. Hungry, with only a few biscuits and sardines eaten since breakfast, they ate all they had. The Doctor led on down. What had been straightforward climbing in the morning with obvious holds posed some problems. Often holds could not be seen until they had committed themselves to a lower position. It was 8:00pm when they left the rocks, but a good moon illuminated their path homeward, reaching camp at 9:40pm.

The Doctor was in need of some treatment, as all the rockwork had worn his fingers bare of skin, and Alec Graham bandaged them for him. He remarked that the plaster could afford better friction if it was applied sticky side out. The Reverend Newton had holes of a different sort: Alec Graham threatened to photograph him, several day's beard on his face, and old dungarees in need of many patches.

After climbing Mount Douglas, they descended the glacier in threatening weather to get more food and to enjoy the hospitality of the Williams family at Weheka. Content with their achievements in three fine days, they were happy for it to rain for a few. They were back in the top camp on 3 February. Snow had plastered Douglas Peak in their absence, and damaged their high camp. Repairs to the shelter and the drying out of gear had to be done before any climbing.

Their next objective was the beautiful Mount Torres, a peak which is a continuation

---

235. Alec Graham & Jim Wilson, op. cit. p73.

of the western arête of Tasman, lying between the Fox and Balfour Glaciers.[236] It is the highest mountain west of the Main Divide, and the only one entirely in Westland over 10,000 feet. That, and the views it afforded of La Perouse and the head of the Balfour were their reasons for this objective.

With the last quarter of the moon as a guide they set off at 3:40am from their camp on the Pioneer Ridge on 4 February. Cloud over the sea warned them of the possibility of fog later on, so Alec carefully marked their tracks in the hard snow with holes from his axe. They made good time across the Fox névé and began climbing up towards the saddle, now named Katies Col, at 4:55am. An hour later they were on the saddle where they had a second breakfast. Finding a route up to the rocks on the arête was difficult. After a few false leads they found a twenty metre couloir which took them on to the rocky part, and then the arête. Snow conditions were better on the Fox side of the ridge and it required negotiating some slabby rock and two gendarmes. From here there were two snow arêtes, the first taking considerable time to negotiate as it was new snow on old. Alec Graham led the Doctor and Mr Newton to the summit, which was reached at 12:15pm. Hands were shaken all round for the fourth first ascent of the trip. The two photographers pulled smaller cameras from out of their swags, and captured the moment, before quickly heading back down to the rocks to get out of the bitter wind for lunch.[237]

The descent and the plod in soft snow back to the top camp took seven and a half hours. The anticipated fog added a degree of trepidation to the névé crossing, until they picked up the trail left by Alec in the morning. Camp was reached at 8:40pm.

It drizzled the following day. Rev Newton spent it darning his holy pants by sewing a sugar sack into the seat. He had to use woollen thread unravelled from a pair of socks discarded by Herman Osmers. On 6 February they checked out the route to Pioneer Pass. Dr Teichelmann's holidays were coming to an end, so he decided to cross the Divide to The Hermitage and return home via Christchurch after having a look at the Christchurch Exhibition. Although Newton doesn't mention it in his diary, it is highly likely that his thoughts that night reflected on the climbing partnership that was coming to its end. Tomorrow would be the last day together for Newton, Graham and Teichelmann as climbers.

---

236. Ibid. p72.
237. Newton Diaries.

The night was hot and they got very little sleep, probably due to being confined to the pit for the previous two days. At midnight they all had a brew, and just when they were nodding off at 1:30am the alarm rang. Alec Graham recalls an uncharacteristic, but mild oath from the Doctor. "Damn that alarm," he muttered.[238] At 4:00am they left for Pioneer Pass, and due to excellent snow conditions, reached it in under two hours.

High camp on Pioneer Ridge before the first ascents of Mt Douglas and Mt Torres

As is quite common at that time of year, they had trouble with route finding around large bergschrunds, and were constantly threatened by ice avalanches. At first they couldn't see anything below, as a large cornice overhung the face and cut it off from view. The only possible site found for crossing the schrund on the eastern slope was directly in the firing line of some massive icicles under the face of Mount Haast. The risks were considered, and it was decided that they would try it, as it was early in the day, and the sun had not yet loosened the icicles' grip on the cornice. Roped together, Newton led off down the slope. He was uneasy, as the snow was loose and new, and just sitting on old hard pack. A recipe for avalanches. Progress was slow, as steps had to be cut through into the solid ice beneath. When he had reached what he thought was a safe stance, he set up a belay close to the upper lip of the schrund. Ice was already beginning to hiss down the slope from above. Newton's nervousness was justified: a large piece thudded into his shoulder with such force and pain that he thought his collarbone was broken.

Below the schrund was a substantial snow basin that provided a reasonably safe runout, should they fall and slide in their leap over this yawning maw. Alec Graham removed

238. Alec Graham & Jim Wilson, op.cit p73.

his pack, containing food and sleeping bags, so he would be free for step-cutting. He threw it over the schrund, but it rolled the wrong way, and went tumbling down the slopes to disappear in the next large crevasse. Newton tried to shelter behind the Doctor's pack. As Dr Teichelmann was the lightest, it was decided to lower him down. He claimed later that they just 'threw him over' in their haste to escape. They were now under constant bombardment from falling ice and it would've taken just one large piece to kill a person.

The Doctor slipped on landing, and rolled down into the crevasse. Fortunately, he was safe on a shelf inside it. The other two lowered their packs and axes down to him. Alec was next, but his hesitation was annoying Newton, who told him to hurry up. He too slipped on landing, winding himself and cutting his mouth and lip. When Newton finally stood on the edge of the precipice, he realized the cause of the trepidation: it was nearly five metres down to the mound below. "I can see now why you paused here!" he called down to Alec. But it had to be done, so plucking up courage, he leaped out. His landing was safe, but he lost his hat in flight. It was now 7:30am.

By walking along the bottom of the schrund, they eventually found a route out. They hurried down to the next slot to look for the missing pack. Fortunately the upper side sloped away sufficiently for Alec to lower Newton down 50 feet until he could see it. He then cut steps down towards it, but feared that the chips of ice would dislodge it and send it out of reach. Just in time, he hooked it with his axe. Another hour had passed.

It had been a tough morning, but there were laughs all round over the number of incidents. From here the route took them over Haast Ridge into the Grand Plateau and on to Glacier Dome, reaching it at 2:10pm. They then descended to Haast Bivouac where Newton and Graham left their packs, as they would return this way in a few days' time. Several hours later they reached Ball Hut.[239]

At Ball Hut, a young New Zealander James Robert Dennistoun, then 24, was deeply impressed by the arrival of Teichelmann and party.

Thursday 7th February 1907

" Mr. Newton, Dr. Teichelmann and Alex Graham all turned up there too, all

239. Ibid, p73.

great climbers and have been out 5 weeks this year and done 5 virgin peaks and had great adventures; especially that day coming over a dangerous pass they had an awful time (Pioneer Pass). Newton is a fine person, has done Mount Cook.

I would love to do some big climbs!"[240]

After a night at Ball Hut the trio reached The Hermitage where Newton and Teichelmann were in their element, being sophisticated men of the world. Names and occupations were important to Newton, and he recorded details meticulously in his diary. It seems that Teichelmann spent much of his time promoting the beauty of the West Coast. "The Doctor fell in for a lot of good natured teasing about his praise for his beloved West Coast scenery," writes Alec Graham.[241]

James Robert Dennistoun

While Teichelmann was in Christchurch, Newton and Graham pushed back over Pioneer Pass in bad weather and down to Chancellor Hut. The pair went on to climb Haast, Lendenfeld, Bristol Top and Conway Peak, all first ascents.[242] They crossed Newton Pass into the Franz Josef névé at 2:00am on 28 February, and thence back to Waiho via the Graham Saddle route past St Mildred Peak, Goatpath, and down Rope Creek.

It must have been with a heavy heart that Alec Graham said goodbye to Rev Newton at Waiho. Later that year Newton returned to England, thus ending a superb list of climbing feats by the greatest climbing trio in the history of New Zealand mountaineering.

Apart from exploring a large amount of virgin territory, the intensity and enormity of Newton,

240. Dennistoun/Mannering. *The Passes & Peaks of J.R.D.* JRD Publication, 1999
241. Alec Graham and Jim Wilson, op.cit.
242. Newton Diaries, 1907.

Teichelmann and the Graham brothers climbing in the period 1902 to 1907 was phenomenal. During six annual trips into the mountains, they had crossed four passes for the first time, made twelve first ascents and the third ascent of Mount Cook.

One wonders as to the depth and breadth of topics they covered during the hundreds of days they spent together under canvas or in bivouacs. In situations more intimate than living in trenches, barriers come done and secrets and weaknesses are difficult to hide. On Teichelmann's army records and death certificate his religion is recorded as a rationalist. I interviewed a number of people about his religion and Hec Davidson said, "The Mountains were Teichelmann's gods." Dorothy Fletcher believes he was brought up in such a very strict manner by his missionary father that he was probably was put off by an over-zealous dad. There is something intriguing about an Anglican minister forming a close relationship with a rationalist doctor. Alec Graham refers to many intense discussions around the campfire, in huts and tents on religion.

Hugh Logan writing in his book *Great Peaks of New Zealand* said,

"The most notable successes were those of the Rev. H. E. Newton, Dr Teichelmann and the Graham brothers between 1902 and 1905, [*mistake, should be* 1907] from the West Coast. Though Teichelmann was the first in the field it was Newton who was the driving force. This party holds a record second to none in our history, and it must be remembered that the Grahams gained the experience, for the great guides they became, from these expeditions."[243]

Later in the year, Teichelmann found some time to traverse part of the Kaiser Fritz Range with the Rev. Kemp and Alec Graham. Starting at Waiho then the trudge up the bush fringed track to the Franz Josef Glacier, 3 km up the Glacier and then up the leg-breaking rock gullies past Castle Rocks over the still un-named peak to Mt. Moltke, Mt. Anderegg, Mt. Roon and finally onto Mt Bismark. Mts. Bismark and Roon were first ascents.

With Newton back in England, it is likely that Teichelmann saw this primarly as a

243. Hugh Logan. *Great Peaks of New Zealand*, John MacIndoe, 1991. p68.

photographic trip with the Fritz Range commanding superb views from Elie de Beaumont and beyond in the north, and nearly all the 3,000 metre peaks in New Zealand as far south as La Perouse. Photographs taken on this trip are scattered through various collections in New Zealand

The peaks of the Fritz Range on the skyline with Tatare Saddle foreground

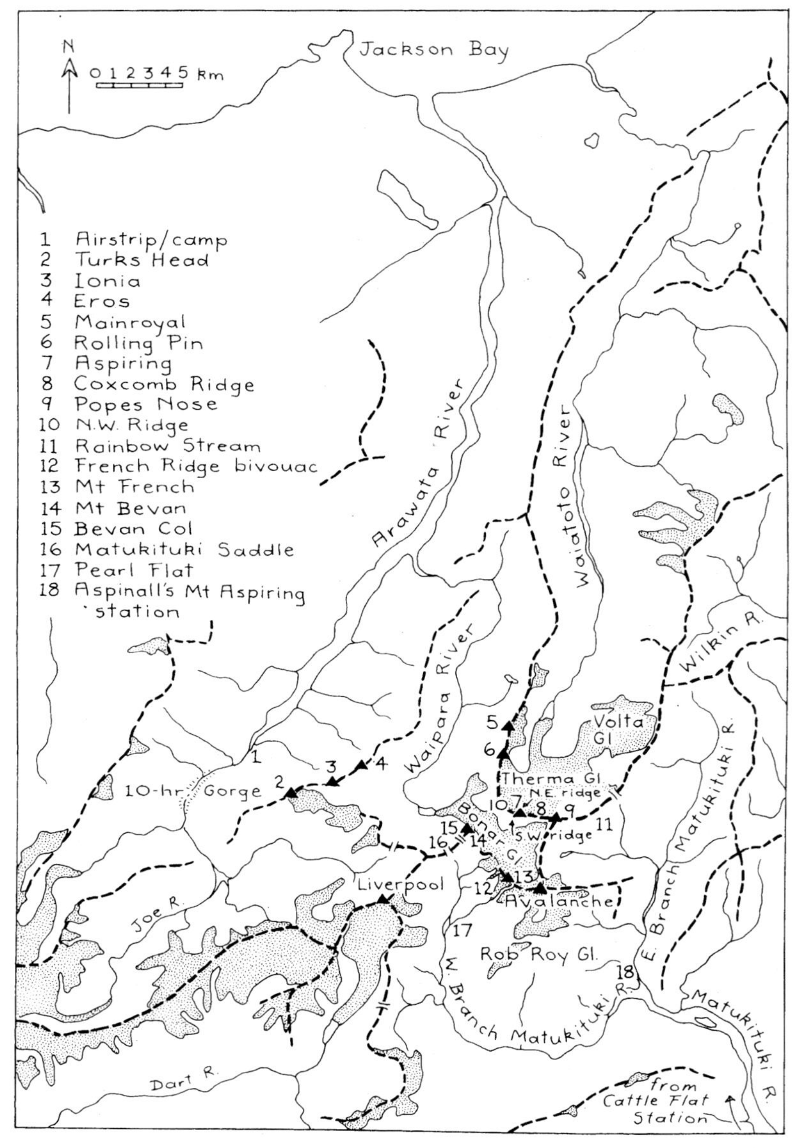

Waiatoto region

1908 The toughest yet - Waiatoto

While The New Zealand Alpine Club was in recess, Dr Teichelmann, Alec and Peter Graham became the experts on New Zealand Mountaineering and received countless letters from Government Ministers and Departments, and from a growing number of young men wishing to take up mountaineering.

From E. Teichelmann, Hokitika to JRD (John Robert Dennistoun), 21st November 1907

I shall be pleased to give you any information I can. The ointment is made of Lanoline with as much Zinc Carbonate rubbed into it will as conveniently hold. A chemist will do it for you.

I don't think there are sleeping bags to be got in the country but you can hire them from the Hermitage as well as ice picks, snow glasses and a rope.

We make our own sleeping bags out of oiled linen ticking, they take about a month to dry.

All other things we get from Switzerland.

I have seen your boots in the making and supplied the nails for them.

Write to Peter Graham for anything you want, the Dept lets them out on hire.[244]

In a letter from Peter Graham to JRD 5th December 1907

---

244. Dennistoun/Mannering, op.cit.

"Sleeping bags; I think you could easily make one yourselves by using light traveling ruff or kapok quilt sewn up the one side, using an oiled calico bag, such as Dr. Teichelmann and the Rev Newton use on the West Coast."

Same letter "All the other equipment such as ice-axes and alpine rope I am afraid is not obtainable in New Zealand and it would be necessary to send to Switzerland for them. The best axe maker is Fritz Jorg, Bernese Oberland, Grindelwald, Switzerland."[245]

Dr Teichelmann traveled south by ship and took this photo of the Southern Alps from the Tasman Sea.

Doctor Teichelmann departed from Hokitika aboard the small coastal ship, the S.S. Jane Douglas at 8:30pm on 17 January, 1908. This coastal boat ran two monthly trips as far south as Jackson's Bay, delivering mail and supplies to remote communities. After a difficult and tiring year, it must have been a relief for him to have a break from his hectic life as Medical Superintendent.

Aboard he had notes from the diary Charlie Douglas had given him on his trips up the Waiatoto Valley. The following day Teichelmann was moved to write about the land that was so special to him:

"On the way down the coast the steamer is never very far out at sea, and the great mountain ranges forming the Southern Alps present one of the greatest sights imaginable. The Franz Josef and Fox Glaciers are seen falling from the summits of the main range almost down to sea level, passing great rocky peaks, and ending in forest of tropical luxuriance. Prominent among the peaks visible from the sea are

245. Ibid

Mounts Cook, Tasman, Elie de Beaumont, and Sefton, the latter showing up particularly well."[246]

Next morning the ship called at Bruce Bay, then Paringa, before spending a night at anchor in Jackson's Bay. The next day Dr Teichelmann disembarked at Okuru, which was some twenty miles from the mouth of the Waiatoto, and the nearest landing spot. Alec Graham and Dennis (Din) Nolan were up the Waiatoto at the time cutting a track. With the help of Matt Nolan, the Doctor used pack horses to carry the expedition's food and equipment from Okuru to Eggling's old homestead, which served as a campsite, some two and a half miles up the Waiatoto valley. 'Prettily situated on the bank of the river, it has some good grass paddocks about it, but it is chiefly remarkable for the number and violence of the mosquitoes that infest it'.[247]

Alec Graham and Din Nolan spent several days cutting a track to within six miles of the Therma Glacier. This is where the river becomes steeper and gorge-infested, the lower 34 miles falling gently through the mountains.

Teichelmann suffered some distress at the state of the track. This was not because of personal discomfort, or even out of concern for the horses. It was due to his imagination, wondering what was happening to his cameras, strapped to the sides of the horses. Every time a horse tried to force a path between trees, he winced.

At one point the river had to be crossed to avoid some bluffs. A dubious craft of vaguely aquatic construction and Nolan lineage was the only option for ferrying the packs. To postpone an imminent submarine destiny, the obvious holes were caulked with sacking and grass. Scrub and branches were laid in the bilges to try to keep the load above water level. Propulsion was one broken oar, so the Doctor paddled furiously on one side, countered on the other by the swift current. A hasty landing and exit was made just as the packs began to float on the rising contents. Matt Nolan crossed with the horses further down stream. A few days later Teichelmann and Matt Nolan teamed up with Alec and Din at the base camp. Matt then returned home with some of the horses. They were

246. NZAJ, 1935. 'The Waiatoto Valley', Dr E. Teichelmann. p19.
247. Ibid p 20.

fortunate in having Charlie Douglas's diaries with them for he had expressed regret at having chosen the right bank of the river instead of the left (western bank). Teichelmann's party took Douglas's advice.

Packing supplies up the lower Waiatoto Valley

When inspecting the equipment Teichelmann had brought, Alec Graham got quite a shock to see the Doctor's supply of cameras and photographic equipment. There was the familiar full plate and small film camera, but in addition to these he had a fairly large Panorama camera and a Stereoscopic, both fairly bulky.

"Do you think there are too many, Alec? You know, Newton is not with us this year and we can play round with them to our heart's content," said the Doctor.[248]

Here we get a brief glimpse into Teichelmann's inner feelings on Newton, his former climbing companion. The exploration, the mapping, the photography, a little botanizing and the comfortable camp were important to the Doctor, but when traveling with Newton, a much younger and often impatient man, with his eyes always looking for another summit to 'knock off, " he wasn't always able to travel at a caravan pace. With Alex Graham and Din Nolan, he was able to slow down and absorb all around him and play with his cameras.

On 22 January, still with pack horses, they continued up the Waiatoto. The pack horses were dispensed with by 25 January and from there the men carried heavy loads up the valley, which become increasingly difficult to travel. Charlie Douglas had written about the difficulties of the upper Waiatoto:

"Altogether, this has been one of the roughest days' traveling I have had for years, & no one but a Lunatic will ever visit the Therma Glacier twice, unless a track is cut, which certainly wouldn't be a very hard job, if it was taken up the other side - the Western side of the Moraine."[249]

Three days later, Alec and Din reached the snout of the Therma Glacier and reported there would be no problems in finding a camp site and that Mount Aspiring looked beautiful, but unpromising from a climber's point of view.[250] Here Teichelmann differs from Alec in his report. Alec claims that the north-west ridge looked encouraging, as the obvious route with no technical difficulties.[251] The advance party returned to join up with the Doctor who had been using to advantage the opportunity to record the incredible beauty on film. Having found a dry, spacious rock shelter close to the terminal face of the glacier, they amused themselves for a few wet days.

The last day of January dawned clear, and the party swagged through the upper river gorge, and set up a high camp on reaching the glacier's snout.

---

248. Alec Graham & Jim Wilson, op cit
249. John Pascoe. *Mr Explorer Douglas*, A.H. & A.W. Reed, 1957. p134.
250. NZAJ, 1935. 'The Waiatoto Valley', Dr E. Teichelmann. p 23.
251. Alec Graham & Jim Wilson. op. cit., p85.

Base Camp on the Therma Glacier

Here Teichelmann had his first full view of Mount Aspiring from the terminus of the Therma Glacier upwards. He was as inspired as the first explorer Charlie Douglas had been and who described it 'as being among the grandest and most magnificent scenery he had known.'[252]

While Din Nolan set up base camp, Alec and Teichelmann went up to the cirque and found the rocky cliffs impenetrable. They decided the thousand-metre-high right-hand icefall was out, so the only option was up the left-hand icefall.

After a comfortable night's sleep they set off early on 1 February. Dr Teichelmann describes the route:

'We made a vain attempt to get through the left icefall, tried the rocks in one place but found them smooth and ice worn, and so decided to retrace and ascend a rocky peak at our left which formed the shoulder to Glacier Dome, a peak on the divide some distance north of Aspiring.'[253]

At 3:30pm, they reached the summit of Glacier Dome. From here they had a superb view of Mount Aspiring. The Doctor felt it could possibly take a week to climb Mount Aspiring, and with his holidays drawing to a close, he decided to return to Hokitika. He was delighted with the time he had devoted to photographing much of this virgin country, and knew his contribution would add to Charlie Douglas' survey work.

Often it takes another mountaineer to put their feat into perspective.

---

252. John Pascoe. op.cit, p134.
253. NZ Alpine Journal, 1935. 'The Waiatoto Valley', Dr E. Teichelmann. p 24.

Mt. Aspiring from the Therma Glacier

When in 1945, Paul Powell, John Sage, Earle Riddiford and Colin Marshall made the first high level traverse of the Volta and the Therma Glaciers under the North Face of Mount Aspiring, they looked down over the hanging icecliffs into the Waiatoto Valley far below... Powell wrote of their feelings in his book, 'Men Aspiring:'

'We had been lucky. Others had planned and tried and failed; we were in their place. I remembered how, 37 years before, Alex Graham, Dennis Nolan and Ebenezer Teichelmann, with his beard and squeaky voice, and plate camera, had reached the upper part of the Waiatoto River after days of Westland swagging. They had made the first ascent of Glacier Dome, noted the route round Aspiring we had later followed, but had to retreat down the Waiatoto ...'

Alec Graham picked out a route on Aspiring and told the Doctor he felt they should have another attempt at it. Back at camp that night he raised the issue again with Teichelmann. Alec Graham recalled the moment:

> 'The Doctor looked at me for a long time with a look I knew so well and then he said, 'I have been thinking over it a lot. I want to stay and can quite imagine how you feel, but Alec, our work in life is the most important thing and I have promised to be home at a certain date. If there is a change in the weather we could easily be flood-bound for a week in this valley, and even when I get out to Okura [Okuru] I

Icefall between Mt. Aspiring and Stargazer from Glacier Dome shoulder.

still have five days travelling and a lot of river to ford before I can get back to Hokitika and could easily be held up at some of the rivers on the way. I have thoroughly enjoyed our trip up this valley, it has been most interesting, but as far as Aspiring is concerned we must consider this as a reconnaissance trip, it will still be there to come back to another year.'[254]

They left supplies and equipment there for another trip, but sadly it was never made.

A letter from Alec Graham to John Robert Dennistoun, dated March 18th 1908, expresses his disappointment

"Dr Teichelmann and myself also had a disappointment this year in not being able to climb Aspiring; were not indeed able to make an attempt on it as we found on reaching the head of the Waiototo River, which has its source from the snowfields on the western slopes of Aspiring, that we were cut off from the peak by a rock wall, swept by avalanches from a high snowfield which skirted the base of the peak.

... The Waiototo valley is very beautiful but seems almost never ending when one is traveling up with a heavy swag (it) being nearly forty miles long. It is very much out (of) the way, our high camp being about 50 miles from the nearest homestead.

The Dr traveled nearly five hundred miles, mostly on horseback by the time he had returned to his home in Hokitika."

---

254. Alec Graham & Jim Wilson. op.cit. pp87, 88.

Avalanche off Stargazer.

Alec Graham traveled back to Waiho with Dr Teichelmann where they met Mr Greville and a survey party carrying out a topographical survey of the Franz Josef Glacier region. The Doctor and Alec accompanied the party to the top of Alee's Knob, where Mr Greville gave the name 'Ebenezer' to the next peak along the ridge towards Mount Moltke. Teichelmann was much amused. "Fancy a peak being saddled with a name like Ebenezer," he chuckled.[255]

Many years later the great English mountaineer H. E. L Porter wrote of Teichelmann's 1908 Waiatoto journey:

'Before 1910 Dr Teichelmann and Alec Graham tried to attack from the west via the Waiototo [sic] valley, but so laborious and prolonged were their struggles with the bush that they had no time left to tackle the Alpine problems above.'[256]

255. Ibid, p89.
256. John Pascoe *Unclimbed New Zealand*, Allen and Unwin, p190.

1909 Climbs from the Tasman Glacier

As the population of the Hokitika area and South Westland gradually increased, Westland Hospital grew with it to provide a comprehensive medical service. Dr Teichelmann's work load and involvement in other voluntary organisations also seemed to increase. In 1909 his alpine holiday was shorter than usual.

The weather was unsettled in early February so they used the time around Waiho with guide Alec Graham by spending a few days photographing the area, until the weather improved. For this trip, they planned to go up Goat Path, cross Graham Saddle and on to The Hermitage. On their way up Goat Path Ridge they found a tin of milk and another of pineapple that Teichelmann and Newton had stashed under a rock in 1902.[257]

At The Hermitage the Doctor was delighted to meet Dr Vollman, an archaeologist from Peru who was a member of the Swiss and Austrian Alpine Clubs. The two doctors enjoyed each other's company, and it was by no accident that Dr Vollman and his guide Peter Graham, Dr Teichelmann and Alec Graham, Darby Thomson and his two male clients, all arrived at Malte Brun Hut together. You can envisage the scene at Malte Brun Hut as they downed countless cups of tea; Vollman and Teichelmann discussing 'worldly matters' and switching from German to English at will, the three West Coast guides talking of climbing, their homes and families on the West Coast, while Thomson's clients wondered what they had struck.[258]

---

257. Alec Graham & Jim Wilson. op.cit. p 91.
258. Peter Graham, op.cit.

Early next morning, 15 February, 1909, the two doctors with the Graham brothers as guides set out for Mount Green. Darby Thomson and clients accompanied them until they turned left off Tasman Glacier for the ridge onto Mount Green. Darby and party headed for Hochstetter Dom.

Mount Cook and the old Hermitage

For Teichelmann it must have been one of his most enjoyable days in the Southern Alps. It was a beautiful day with not a breath of wind. Using the narrow arête from the Tasman Valley, they climbed Mount Green, where Teichelmann took particular interest in the view down into the Callery Valley, one of the most impenetrable on the West Coast. Mount Walter looked more comfortable for dining, so they climbed that also, crossing the col and ascending its north-eastern arête. A pleasant social chat ensued. The Doctor was now fifty years old and in good health. With him were his two protégé, Alec and Peter Graham, who he had nurtured and encouraged to be mountain guides. Peter Graham couldn't help but notice his joy:

'The two doctors were greatly enjoying the leisurely climb, and both being keen photographers, they were making the best use of their time on both peaks. We boiled the alpine cooker for tea on the top of Mount Walter, and had a picnic lunch, spending more than an hour there admiring the view of the Tasman Valley and the surrounding peaks, with Malte Brun rising grandly across the valley. My eye was ever drawn towards the view to the west, for immediately below were the Spencer

Glacier, the western slopes of Elie de Beaumont, and the camping spot of that expedition years before when with Dr Teichelmann and Arthur Woodham, I had made my first real contact with the mountains.'[259]

An exciting glissade took them quickly to the Tasman Glacier and the Malte Brun Hut. That night Dr Vollmann entertained all residents with a description of archaeological work in an old Inca cemetery in Peru.[260]

Teichelmann had been thinking about a quick trip to have a look at the virgin peak Mount Aspiring from the eastern approach, the peak that he had unsuccessfully tried to climb from the west the previous year. Teichelmann wanted to climb this peak so much, but his leave was running out and he had to give the idea up.

In writing to Jim Dennistoun on 5 April 1909, Alec Graham gives further background.

"Dr Teichelmann's holiday was somewhat spoilt by unfavourable weather at the beginning which delayed our crossing for a week. If we had arrived at the Hermitage in time he had intended going down to Lake Wanaka and having another look at Aspiring, but being delayed so long made it impossible."[261]

For Dr Teichelmann it was a quick trip back to the Hermitage and then home to Hokitika via the Copland Pass.

A few months later, in the depths of a West Coast winter, Jack Clarke wrote to Alec Graham, saying that Mr Earle and Captain Head were planning a trip up the Matukituki valley with the first ascent of Mount Aspiring as the key objective. Alec Graham sought advice from Teichelmann and describes his feelings at the time.

'This was very exciting news and I was keen to go, the only sad bit about it was that it was not with the Little Doctor. I spoke to him about the offer, and he said I would be very foolish to refuse the opportunity and wished me the best of luck.[262]

259. Ibid, p180.
260. Ibid.
261. Dennistoun/Mannering, op.cit.
262. Alec Graham & Jim Wilson..op.cit. p97.

NEW ZEALAND ILLUSTRATED, THE CHRISTMAS NUMBER OF THE WEEKLY PRESS

THE MALTE BRUN RANGE, LOOKING ACROSS THE TASMAN GLACIER FROM THE LOWER PART OF THE BALL PASS

BOOTS FOR ALPINE CLIMBING.

THE HOOKER CAGE.

INTERIOR OF THE MALTE BRUN HUT, THE HIGHEST INHABITED BUILDING IN NEW ZEALAND.

THE HIGHEST INHABITED BUILDING IN NEW ZEALAND—THE MALTE BRUN HUT, 500FT. ABOVE THE TASMAN GLACIER, 5700FT. ABOVE SEA LEVEL.

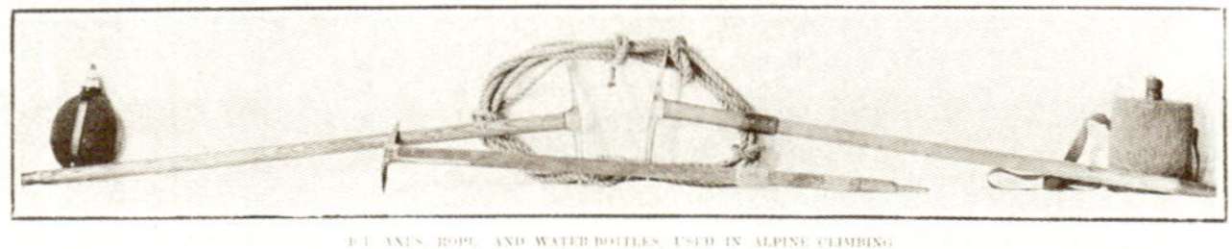

ICE AXES, ROPE, AND WATER BOTTLES USED IN ALPINE CLIMBING.

A full page montage from the 1904 New Zealand Illustrated the Christmas Number of the Weekly Press showing the Malte Brun Range and views of the exterior and interior of the Malte Brun Hut.

Hugh Logan writes of Graham's regret of going without Teichelmann:

'But to his sorrow, it was without his friend Teichelmann... It seems likely that Graham accepted the offer rather reluctantly. He would have preferred to be with Teichelmann, and did not hold Head, and especially Earle, in very high regard. Earle had earned the generous-spirited West Coaster's contempt for selfish behaviour when he, Head, Alec and Peter Graham, Jack Clarke and Darby Thomson had been caught the previous summer on low rations in the upper Landsborough to the North.'[263]

Fortunately Earle withdrew from the climb of Aspiring with which Head, Graham and Clarke did a spectacular first ascent from via the Western Face.

This view that not only Alec Graham, but Teichelmann didn't have a great deal of respect for Head, is supported by Dorothy Fletcher who heard this first hand from her father, Alec.

---

263. Hugh Logan.op.cit. pp68,69.

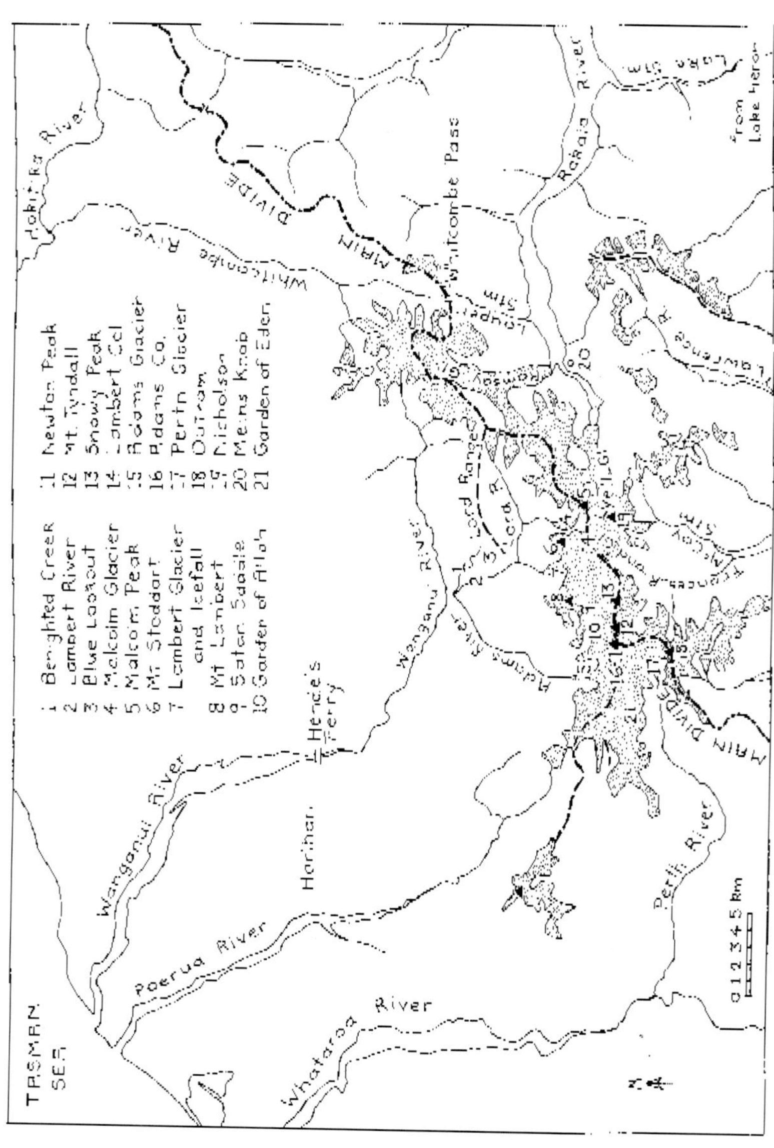

The Wanganui River and the Rakai River Headwaters

1910 *Rakaia and Whitcombe Pass*

Teichelmann was 51 years of age when he took on this major expedition up the Rakaia, He knew he would need to be in peak fitness for this transalpine journey. He headed for the Franz Josef Glacier region to get fit, and wrote to Newton that "I played about at the Franz Josef for a time and had two unsuccessful attempts to cross Graham Saddle... and then crossed by the Copland."[264]

The playing about at Franz Josef resulted in a shortening of the route up the Franz Josef Glacier to Graham Saddle and into Canterbury. Newton recorded that 'this route into Canterbury has been in use for a good number of years, and it was only in January last year (1910) that a still further shortening of the route was made by a party comprising of Mr L. Lindon (Geelong Grammar School), Dr E. Teichelmann and Alex Graham. Whilst this route, details of which lack of space forbids, is undoubtedly shorter, there is a disadvantage entailed in having to occupy a camp site where there is no firewood.'[265]

Once again in the Mount Cook area Ebenezer choose Mount Chudleigh as a warm-up climb, with guides Alec and Peter Graham. They achieved the first ascents of the low and middle peak on 19 February, 1910.[266] The Doctor wasn't very impressed by the rock, which he described as 'rotten loose rock very unlike Malte Brun'.[267]

---

264. Newton Diaries. p147.
265. Ibid.
266. Johannes. C. Andersen, *Jubilee History of South Canterbury*, Whitcombe and Tombs,1916
267. Newton Diaries

Competition in mountaineering has been alive long before the first ascent of the Matterhorn and it was obviously alive in well in this era, and mountaineers were always trying to find out what the others were up to. Jim Dennistoun, who was climbing in the Mount Cook region around the same time with guide Jack Clarke, writes in his diary 28 February, 1910: "We learn that Dr Teichelmann and Alec Graham are coming to have a go at Arrowsmith from the front, via Mount Somers."[268] Dennistoun, always generous in spirit but territorial in nature, was watching his patch of the Southern Alps very carefully, hoping many of those celestial virgin peaks would remain that way until he attempted them himself.

Alec Graham and Dr Teichelmann traveled from Mount Cook to Ashburton. From there they took a train to Mount Somers, purchased food and supplies, and hired a trap to take them to Lake Heron Station. The pair used horses to reach the first shepherd's hut and the next day, packed up to a camp under Mein's Knob. For five days it rained and the pair were forced to shift camp to higher ground. During the incessant rain, they climbed the Knob with only occasional glimpses of the Lyell Glacier and the surrounding mountains.

During a respite Graham and Teichelmann crossed the Rakaia and camped on a spur at the junction of the Louper. The rain continued but they travelled up the left bank of the Rakaia and got onto the Ramsay Glacier at its terminus. They now knew the route up the Rakaia to the snout of Lyell Glacier, but continuous rain hampered further exploration. They returned to Hokitika via Whitcombe Pass and Kowhitirangi farm settlements. Teichelmann wrote, 'Having failed in this attempt, we decided to tackle the region from the Wanganui in the following season.'[269]

As Graham and Teichelmann were overdue, they met a search party on the way out.

'The gratifying news of the safety of Dr Teichelmann and Guide Alex Graham was received in Hokitika yesterday afternoon from Koiterangi [sic] shortly before five o'clock, and about eight o'clock the Doctor and his guide arrived home, being accompanied as a

268. Dennistoun/Mannering, op.cit.

269. NZAJ, 1923. 'The Relation of the Rakaia and Rangitata on the East to the Wanganui and Wataroa on the West,' Dr E. Teichelmann.

Few photographs were taken on this trip. Barron Canyon, Price's River, Upper Whitcombe

bodyguard by the party who had left town earlier for the purpose of proceeding up the Whitcombe Pass to assist in the search for the party in accordance with Guide Peter Graham's suggestion.'[270]

But not only were fears held for the Doctor and his party from the West Coast side of the mountain, but on Tuesday 15 March Jim Dennistoun writes in his diary from Mount Somers on the eastern side of the Alps, "Now we know that Teichelmann is safe, did nothing, and finally got through Whitcombe Pass. (He and Alec were after Arrowsmith and a Lyell/Wanganui Pass)"[271] The 'did nothing' perhaps was indicating relief that the unclimbed peaks were still inviolate.

There are no exact dates for the return of Teichelmann to Hokitika, or records of Teichelmann meeting with recently retired Chief Surveyor G. J. Roberts to share details of his journey. But his return would have been somewhere around 10 March, 1910. It is safe to assume Teichelmann would have talked to Roberts, and it is easy to picture them poring over photographs, and Teichelmann taking advice for his next trip to the head of the Wanganui. Although Roberts died before he could witness the results, the Doctor was inspired to unravel the remaining mysteries of the Upper Wanganui and the Lambert Glacier.

Teichelmann's article in the 1923 New Zealand Alpine Journal throws light on his relationship with Roberts :

> 'The late Mr J. G. [sic] Roberts, Chief Surveyor and Commissioner of Crown Lands for Westland, always took interest in our climbing expeditions in Westland, and was helpful in supplying detail maps and advice. He expressed a desire that we should explore the headwaters of the Wanganui, particularly the Lambert branch, stating that the Survey Department was very uncertain about the topography of that region. In compliance with this desire, I decided to organise an expedition up the Rakaia from the east, to endeavour to cross the divide in that region, and come down the Lambert and Wanganui to the Coast.'[272]

---

270. West Coast Times. Undated cutting.
271. Dennistoun/Mannering, op.cit.
272. NZAJ 1923, p175

1911 Unraveling mysteries of the Lambert and Lord

Jock Adamson had persuaded Alec Graham and the Doctor that horses could pack provisions and gear up to the forks where the Wanganui meets the branches of the Lambert and Adams. On 25 January, 1911, they left Hendes Ferry for the Upper Wanganui. The rivers must have been running high with snowmelt, because they had only gone two and a half kilometres to Canopy Bluff when they found the river was unfordable. Teichelmann sent the horses back and replaced them with 'three stalwart West Coasters': Carl Hende, MacKay and Weller to assist them swagging equipment up river.

The next day the party of five, carrying loads between 23 and 32 kilograms each, tramped up the river until they reached an old geological survey camp site near the junction of the Wanganui and Lambert, on Jones' Flat.

The route was mostly in the riverbed, but some bushbashing was necessary to avoid the bluffs where the river runs in hard against the rock. One porter was almost swept away, probably crossing Hendes Creek, and owed his life to Alec for a swift rescue. The following day they moved up the Lambert to Benighted Creek, where the three stalwarts dropped their loads and returned home. Carl Hende returned a few days later with Jack Clarke.

Clarke joined Teichelmann and Graham, and on 31 January they carried heavy loads up to Blue Lookout, 'an open cave above the head of Benighted Creek and well up on the Lord Range...

Camp at the Wanganui Forks. Mt Stoddard in the background.

This was an old camp-site of Charlie Douglas...'[273] The view from here was spectacular. Below the Wanganui River took a winding course seawards, visible as far as Mount Wilberg, and above, the impassable Lambert Gorge and the towering 300 metre Lambert Icefall dominated. 'Both these views, down the river and up to the mountains, are seen over a foreground of lilies and daisies, with not a *blue* flower among them'.[274] Three days of bad weather passed and on 4 February, they climbed up to the crest of the

273. NZAJ, 1923. 'The Relation of the Rakaia and Rangitata on the East to the Wanganui and Wataroa on the West,' Dr E. Teichelmann. p183.

274. Ibid. p184.

Blue Lookout on the Lord Range

Lord Range and dropped down the other side, hoping to find a route on to the Lambert Glacier above the threatening ice-fall. It seemed the only way was to drop into the Lord riverbed and set up camp on the northern shoulder of Mount Stoddart. On 5 February they descended steeply into the Lord, crossed it, and ascended a creek up Mount Stoddart. Alec had to cut a route for ninety minutes through the sub-alpine scrub 'which tries the temper and patience of a climber more than anything else'.[275] By the morning of 6 February, they climbed and traversed round the shoulder of Mount Stoddart and found an easy descent onto the Lambert Glacier just above the icefall. Teichelmann was thrilled. 'We were now on the high snowfields of the Lambert, and travelling was easy in many directions. Mount Lambert was a glorious sight across the undulating and slightly crevassed snowfields, with the early morning sun producing great contrasts of light and shade.'[276]

It was still early in the morning so they pressed on up the snowfield to the Main Divide, reaching it at 8:00am. Here they had a second breakfast, sunbathed and took a great many photographs. Mountaineer Jim Wilson believes they were on Lambert Col at this point.[277]

The topographical mysteries were slowly being unravelled. Teichelmann describes what he saw from Lambert Col:

275. Ibid. p185.
276. Ibid. p186.
277. Alec Graham & Jim Wilson.op.cit. p105.

Malcolm Peak and the Arrowsmiths from Snowy Peak

'We expected to look down into the Lyell Glacier (Rakaia River) but instead of that we were looking into the Clyde Branch of the Rangitata, which here sends a projection (the Francis Glacier) in the direction of Malcolm Peak, quite cutting off the Lyell from the Lambert snowfields, and saddling over into the basin of the Lord. Opposite us on the left was Mount Nicholson, seen across the Francis Glacier. This was the peak climbed by Dennistoun and party the previous season, and some tributary glaciers came down from its flanks to join the Francis. Looking along the Divide to the south-west a small peak appeared in the skyline, which we thought might be Tyndall.'[278]

278. NZAJ, 1923. p186.

At 9:30am they walked along the Main Divide ridge to find it wasn't Mount Tyndall. They christened it Snowy Peak (2376m) and then carried on the West Coast side of the ridge to record the first ascent of Mount Tyndall (2517m). This was the southern edge of the Garden of Allah Snowfield, known now as John Pascoe Ridge, which they were traversing. From the southern end of Mount Tyndall are twin rocks and from here they got an unimpeded view into the Perth River to the south-west and into the Adams Gorge to the west.

Opposite Mount Tyndall to the west they found the highest unnamed peak in the region. It was obvious Teichelmann and Graham were missing Newton, so in his honour they named the mountain Newton Peak (2543m).

Newton Peak from the South Peak of Tyndall

Newton Peak stands out on its own, away from the Divide. It separates the Garden of Allah from the Garden of Eden Ice Plateau. At 1:00pm the group descended a fairly steep snow slope towards Newton Peak and crossed the saddle between the Adams and Lambert Glaciers, regaining the route they had taken earlier in the day at Mount Stoddart. At 6:00pm they reached their camp.

Jack Clarke and Alec Graham were keen to push off early next morning to climb the beautiful virgin peak of Malcolm (2514m), but Teichelmann asked for a rest. He was now 52 years of age, and had been pushing himself hard on this trip. The next day they had a short outing to the north shoulder of Mount Stoddart, to check the route up Malcolm and take further photographs. Teichelmann was impressed with the thousand-metre high precipice on the north-eastern side of Stoddart, overhanging the Malcolm Glacier.

Malcolm Peak from the north

On Wednesday 8 March they set off as soon as light permitted, descended the gully they had checked out the previous day, then climbed up the Malcolm Glacier with easy traveling to the base of Malcolm Peak. Turning right they kicked steps up a narrow snow couloir. They alternated between rock and snow to provide variety, but eventually they had to cut steps as they climbed higher and the surface hardened. The Divide was mounted near the southern arête of Malcolm. Here they relaxed, and spent an hour and three quarters eating, resting and changing clothes. Teichelmann changed his singlet, a regular habit, which in his words, 'I have always found that a change into a dry singlet when I am wet and cold infuses new vigour into me.'[279]

279. Ibid. p189.

Refreshed, the trio pushed on across a ledge on the western face. It alternated between shingle, snow, good rock and more snow, taking them to the north-western arête and on to the corniced summit. Teichelmann was delighted. He had fulfilled his promise to the late G.J. Roberts, for now, on this auspicious day, 'the weather was now perfect and the views in every direction were magnificent. The whole topography of the region seemed to be laid out before us as if it were a map.'[280] The climb of Malcolm both added to, and confirmed many of the topographical finds of the previous days.

Looking down the Wanganui River

They traversed the peak and descended on steep snow and some rockwork to be near the Divide on the north-east side. Three glissades took them onto the Malcolm Glacier, and they reached camp late in the afternoon. Not content to sit back and savour a highly successful day, they packed up camp and descended to the left bank of the Lord River where they slept on some very soft wet patches of sphagnum moss. Two days later they reached Hendes Ferry, having left a fair amount of food and equipment at each camp. 'We always avoided burdening ourselves with things that might be useful to the next man, and we stowed them as securely as possible, safe from keas, wekas and weather.'[281] Having achieved three first ascents of significant mountains, unravelled the last remaining topographical mystery on the West Coast, and taken vital photographs for the Survey Department, Teichelmann could be justified in praising himself. However, the ever-modest Doctor praised his two guides: 'this was one of the most interesting trips

280. NZAJ, 1923. p189.
281. Ibid. p190.

I have ever made, and it was made comfortable by my two companions. Fortunate indeed is the climber who has Graham and Clark [sic] for his guides.'[282]

Friend and fellow photographer W. A Kennedy spoke of the photographic success of the expedition some 30 later. 'Remarkably fine photographic results were obtained from the heads of the more southerly sub-tributaries of the Big Wanganui, namely the Lord and Lambert, and from the Divide peaks of Malcolm, Snowy and Tyndall, and these photographs later proved of great assistance in the mapping of this country.'[283]

In June that year Alec and Jim Graham purchased Batson's Hotel at Waiho, which saw Alec very busy for the next few years, and restricted the time he could spend mountain guiding with the Doctor.

---

282. Ibid. p190.
283. *Canterbury Mountaineer*, 1936.

1912 From the Footstool to Switzerland

It is difficult to unravel exactly what Dr Teichelmann did with his annual leave in early 1912. Obviously plans had been made, as The West Coast Times of Tuesday 16 January, 1912, announced details of his annual expedition:

> 'Doctor Teichelmann leaves this morning on a trip to the ice regions of South Westland. The Doctor will go as far south as Cooks River and hopes to ascend the Fox Glacier, cross to Canterbury, visit the Hermitage, and return to Westland by way of the Big Wanganui River. Dr Teichelmann will be accompanied by the Reverend C. E. Thorpe an English clergyman, who has been resident in New South Wales for some years and who previously had some Swiss mountain experience. Mr Alexander Graham will act as guide to the party and the trip is expected to occupy about three weeks.'[284]

There is no evidence to suggest he did this full trip.

Although he left Hokitika, Dr Teichelmann was keen to have another fling in the Southern Alps before sailing for Europe. At this time, although Alec Graham was heavily involved in setting up a hotel business, records show that the fourth, fifth and sixth ascents of The Footstool were done on the same day - 3 April, 1912. Dr Teichelmann was in a party with H. Chambers and guides Alec Graham and Jack Clarke and did the fifth ascent. Others on the mountain that day were Mr and Mrs Lindon with guides Darby Thomson and Jack Lippe, and H. F. Wright and J. E. Walker.[285]

---

284. West Coast Times, 1912.
285. Johannes C. Andersen. op.cit..

This was one of the last times Darby Thomson climbed. Tragically Darby was killed, along with two friends, a year after the Doctor returned from Europe.

The Matterhorn

What Mecca is to the Moslem, the Matterhorn is to the mountaineer. Between visits to European and English hospitals, Ebenezer Teichelmann went to Zermatt in early August, 1912. August, in those days, was considered the month for climbing in Switzerland. Rather than take the mountain railway to Gornergrat situated at 3000 metres, the Doctor chose to walk. Here he stayed at the famous Gornergrat Hotel where the English Alpine Club have accommodation reserved for its members and friends. Teichelmann, who became a member of the Alpine Club in 1902, received a warm welcome on his arrival from the Seiler family, who ran the hotel.[286]

---

286. Christchurch Press, 17 January 1913. p7, col 7.

From initial delight to be in the high Swiss Alps with unsurpassed views of the Matterhorn and the other high peaks of the area, frustration set in with the 'exasperating inclemency of the weather.'

An article in the Christchurch Press from an interview he gave on his return said, 'Almost every excursion was abruptly terminated by storms and heavy falls of snow, which drove the explorers back into one of the numerous cabanes or shelters which abound.'[287]

One of the most famous mountain sketches appears in Edward Whymper's *Scrambles Amongst The Alps in the Years 1860-69* of the Matterhorn from near the summit of the Theodule Pass which connects Switzerland to Italy.[288] On one trip, the Doctor reached the Theodule Pass, and would have enjoyed following in the footsteps of the great Edward Whymper. The weather was never good enough to climb the peaks of the Matterhorn and the Zinal Rothhorn, but he managed two other climbs of the Wellenkuppe and Furgengrat.

With appointments to keep, Dr Teichelmann left feeling quite disappointed at not being able to scale the heights of the Matterhorn.

The finale for the Doctor on the day before he left for New Zealand was to lecture on the New Zealand Alps at the Saville Row London headquarters of the English Alpine Club. Using lantern slides to illustrate, he was able to show 'the glories of the New Zealand Alps among whose mighty peaks and flowing glaciers the Doctor had spent so many pleasant days'.[289] But more specifically his talk was on the mountains of the West Coast. All previous lectures on New Zealand presented to the Club had concentrated on the East Coast, the open sheep country and the mountains, wrote Newton some years later.[290]

On his return to New Zealand, he was asked by a reporter from the Christchurch Press how the Swiss Alps compared with the Southern Alps:

'Dr Teichelmann said that the alpine district in the vicinity of the Zermatt appeared

---

287. Ibid.

288. Edward Whymper. *Scrambles Amongst the Alps in the Years 1860 - 69*, John Murray, London. 1871.

289. Christchurch Press, op cit.

290. Newton Diaries.

to him to be less interesting than were the Southern Alps from the Westland side, and more interesting than their Canterbury aspect. It was difficult to make a comparison between the two countries as the mountains of Switzerland and those of New Zealand were so similar, but he would say that there was not a mountain peak in the world comparable to the majesty and splendour of the Matterhorn and he much regretted being unable to make an attempt to scale its frozen heights. Speaking generally, however, the Doctor considered that our Alps compared quite favourably with those of Switzerland. On the Westland side of the Southern Alps the forest is much denser than anything he saw on the Swiss Alps and to his mind the heavy forests added considerably to the ruggedness of our Alps. Of course, on the Canterbury side of Mount Cook the forest was even sparser than that on the Swiss ranges.'[291]

Teichelmann also made another statement which compared the ruggedness of New Zealand's West Coast mountains to the majesty of the Matterhorn.

It is important to put his trip to Europe after twelve years of mountaineering in New Zealand, into some sort of context, for this analytical antipodean had returned to the continent of his parents, where he updated his medical and surgical techniques, and was now an avowed New Zealander in his words, actions, spirit and soul. The passion he had for the West Coast of New Zealand and its rugged landscape bordered on evangelical. He took every opportunity to promote the West Coast first, and New Zealand mountaineering.

Without saying it, he pioneered a theme which many later New Zealand mountaineers made about the chocolate box photographs of the Swiss Alps with its easy access to the rugged mountains, forest to sea of New Zealand Alps where swagging heavy packs for three weeks is the norm. His lecture to the English Alpine Club was the first ever highlighting the remote and rugged character of the West Coast side of the Southern Alps of New Zealand.

He also visited Berlin, Vienna, Birmingham, Dresden and Leipzig during his 1912 trip and although not recorded, it is hard not to think that he didn't seize or engineer an

291. Christchurch Press, op cit.

opportunity as an over zealous promoter of New Zealand, in giving a lecture at the end of a day's learning in a hospital or medical university.

In some lectures he showed slides of the Matterhorn and Everest for contrast with his beloved West Coast Mountains.

The primary role Ebenezer Teichelmann played in pre-first world war New Zealand mountaineering in nurturing Peter and Alex Graham to become skilled mountain guides, and encouraging another prominent West Coast guide, Darby Thomson, and, to start a mountain guiding tradition on the West Coast which has continued and grown during the last century, while exploring many remote valleys and climbing many unclimbed peaks. Equally important was his role in promoting mountaineering when the fledging New Zealand Alpine club, which started in 1891 and continued for less than a decade, before

Mt. Moltke, Mt. Tasman and Aoraki Mt. Cook

drifting into hibernation. The means of promotion were varied; articles that he, and his colleague Newton wrote and beautifully illustrated in the Canterbury Times, New Zealand Illustrated, New Zealand Graphic and photographs in Leonard Cockayne's Geographical Report of the Franz Josef Glacier in 1910, lectures given on the West Coast and Canterbury, his visit and lecture to the English Alpine Club in 1912, his large exhibit of his magnificent photographs at the International Exhibition in 1907, and through clever advocacy.

The way he introduced Mr. T. E. Donne, the Superintendent of the Tourist Department to the Graham brothers in 1903, and networked and advocated to Ministers, with influence, and leading people in Government in Wellington, and overseas dignitaries, for better support for tourism and infrastructure, and facilities.

His lobbying at the Canterbury Progress League meetings, West Coast Acclimatisation Society and municipality and district council meetings, promoted recreation, tourism and improved economies through the judicious use of natural resources, while at the same time talking of his eye witness accounts that whole communities could make sustainable livelihoods from tourism after his visit to Europe. His work in preserving wilderness areas by lobbying for reserves or national park status, was nothing short of revolutionary.

Dr. Teichelmann on top of Mt. Spencer

1914 First ascent of Mount Spencer - three dead

With the latest mountaineering equipment he had bought back from his recent trip to Europe, Ebenezer Teichelmann set out to climb a jewel in West Coast mountains. While the rest of New Zealand fawned over peaks like Cook, Tasman and Aspiring, people who farm or till the land on the Waiho flats, or live at Okarito, see a peak that often looks more spectacular than them all-Mount Spenser. From Canavan's Knob on a clear day, it has the majesty of the Matterhorn, and often framed by rata and its praises sung by tuis, woodpigeons and bellbirds. Teichelmann must have gazed at this peak countless times in the course of his visits to patients and gazed back to Spencer thinking, "I have climbed all the big ones, but are you not a jewel in the crown ? ". Similarly, Alec Graham from the day he first looked at mountain from his remote home at Three Mile, and later Waiho and its environs, must have likewise thought of it as a local guardian, a sentinel.

In late February 1914 at the age of 55, Dr Teichelmann was back climbing on the Franz Josef névé with Alec Graham. They climbed Mount Spencer from Almer Glacier, over the névé of the Franz Josef Glacier to the col north of Mount Spencer, and then on to the summit by the north-eastern arête.[292] This was the 2788 metre peak on the Main Divide near its junction with the Fritz Range; not to be confused with the other Mount Spencer (1648m) not far away on the Burster Range.

Unbeknown to Teichelmann and Alex Graham, while they were on this trip, less than ten kilometres away, on the slopes of Mount Cook, a tragic drama was unfolding on the Linda Glacier.

---

292. Johannes C. Andersen. op.cit.

The Christchurch Press on Saturday, 28 February 1914 ran the following headlines

THE MOUNT COOK TRAGEDY

WITH THE SEARCH PARTY
An appalling avalanche
Party's terrible difficult task

Mr. Dennistoun's narrative

FAIRLIE, February 27

The terrible alpine disaster which has taken the first toll of human life on the slopes of Mount Cook caused great grief at the Hermitage, and cast a deep gloom over the parties of tourists there. The first complete and connected narrative of the disaster that has come from Mount Cook was graphically told to a representative of "The Press" at Fairlie tonight by Mr. James R. Dennistoun.

According to various accounts, Mr, S. L. King, and guides Jock Richmond and Darby Thomson, were killed by an avalanche, at around 5:00pm, on Sunday 22 February, after a successful ascent of Mount Cook.

On Wednesday 25 February, Peter Graham who was a member of the search party "caught sight of a stone, but proved to be one of Richmond's boots, sticking out of a wall of a narrow crevasse. There were piles of ice above the body, which was completely buried... When we finally got the poor, mutilated body clear we found that the rope by which the man had been secured to his companions had been broken clean through by the sharp blocks of ice about six or seven feet behind him."[293]

An entry in the first Defiance Hut book dated 28 February, 1914, confirms that Dr Teichelmann and Alec Graham passed through the hut after their climb of Mount Spencer. It reads:

293. Dennistoun and Mannering, op.cit.

E Teichelmann Hokitika - Glorious weather

A Graham Waiho - first ascent Mount Spencer from Almer[294] However, this correct date in the Defiance Hut book is at odds Johannes Andersen who described their trip as being on 1 March, 1914.

Photo 94 Darby Thomson ((right) the West Coast mountain guide tragically killed on Mount Cook. An earlier photo of him saw milling with Dave Graham on the left..

The Waiho and West Coast community was rocked by the death of Darby Thomson who was a highly competent guide and from a well respected pioneering family.

In a letter to Newton (held in the Hocken library) from Teichelmann, he describes the trip, with comments in brackets by Newton:

'Last February I took my holiday and had to go to Auckland. However I could not resist running down to the Waiho for a short holiday, almost twelve days. I had intended spending a little while up the Fox, but I had not enough time so Alex and I decided to have one climb at the head of the Franz Josef. We camped at the Defiance Hut, then camped again on Almer Rock. From there we skirted round the Mildred Peak spur - low down, went past Mackay Rock, then over a saddle above the Tusk somewhere near where you (H.E.N) and Alex crossed it on your trip from Pioneer Camp to the Waiho (see my trip 1907 - as a matter of fact we went below the Tusk)

294. Defiance Hut Book 1912- 1930. Graham Collection, Hokitika.

After that we crossed another spur of the Divide and reached the Divide immediately under Mount Spencer (presumably N. of it). The ascent of Mount Spencer from this col was not difficult - a little snow and then a very rotten rock arête taking in all 3/4 hour. The summit was very interesting, large rocks loosely filled or rather packed forming a very sharp final ridge, very unsafe to look at (like Conway?) We had a tremendous ducking on our return from Almer Bivouac to the Defiance Hut as well as a bad wet night preceding.'[295]

Lake Mapourika, a pleasant stop for a picnic or a paddle when returning from Franz Josef to Hokitika

This was to be his last climb before he and Alec Graham went overseas to serve New Zealand in the Great War. Arthur P. Harper describes the situation: 'The War, 1914-1918, took many of our active climbers overseas. The absence of Wright, Hugh Chambers, Teichelmann, Talbot, J. R. Dennistoun and Alec Graham, not to mention any others, made a considerable gap in our team.'[296]

A number of their friends both of the cities and the mountains never returned. And many like Jack Clarke that did return, never climbed again seriously through injuries sustained overseas.

The Doctor's climbing career was not yet over, but he had played a very

295. Newton Diaries.

296. A.P. Harper, *Memories of Mountains and Men*, Simpson and Williams Ltd, Christchurch, 1946

important role - that of keeping the new sport of mountaineering alive in New Zealand after the New Zealand Alpine Club went into recess, through regular expeditions, photographs and articles.[297] Through his encouragement and support Alec and Peter Graham became two of the most notable mountain guides in New Zealand, and together they put South Westland on the map as a destination for tourists and mountaineers.

297. Ibid.

1924 Perth River and Sealey Pass

For 13 years Dr Teichelmann had dreamed of completing his 1911 exploratory work up the Wanganui Valley. The war intervened, the influenza epidemic came and his medical duties just didn't give him the time to get away. He was now 65 years of age, an age when most mountaineers have hung up their ice axe and retired to the rocking chair. The year before, 1923, he had written a detailed account in the NZ Alpine Club Journal entitled 'The Relation of the Rakaia and the Rangitata on the East to the Wanganui and Wataroa on the West', which described his 1910 and 1911 expeditions.

In the same journal, preceding Teichelmann's article was an article, 'The Late J. R. Dennistoun's Work and its Value,' by Arthur P. Harper. Both articles have a common map showing the headwaters of the Rakaia, Rangitata, Wanganui and Whataroa Rivers, with the route of Dennistoun's and Teichelmann's routes.[298]

Writing about his 1910 and 1911 expeditions for the 1923 Journal must have fired him up for one last go. In a letter to Newton he says, 'My intention was to try and connect up with the Wanganui trip I made in 1911 - and I chose (as it now turns out) the wrong river for it'.[299]

Teichelmann left sometime late in February 1924, for his last major trip into the Southern Alps. His problem lay in getting a top guide to accompany him. He tried to secure the services of Alec and Peter Graham, but neither was available. Similarly Jack

298. NZAJ, 1923, p168.
299. Letter to Newton, Teichelmann. 6 May 1924. Graham Collection, Hokitika.

Clarke and Collet were unavailable, so the only guide free at that time was Jock Lippe. For a porter he took a local, Harry Butland.

The party of three took pack horses with them on the first day up the Whataroa. At the junction of the Whataroa and Perth Rivers the climbers crossed the footbridge and from there to Harry Heveldt's little shack about four miles up the Perth River on the true left, they had to walk through the 'most awful swamp', which was caused by cattle. The horses sunk in up to their bellies, and the route up the Perth was slow going. 'No one had been up the river as far as Scone Creek for about fifteen years, so that any blaze line that had existed in those times was practically obliterated and we were forced to make our own track up which meant much loss of time and much labour', he wrote to Newton.[300]

Next morning, they followed a semblance of a track for eight miles and from here on they were forced to cut a track through heavy bush. There were a few gravel riverbed sections until they neared the Scone Creek junction. It took Teichelmann and his party two weeks to establish a camp at Scone Creek. For a man of his age spending two weeks hacking a track through virgin bush, mostly in the wet, speaks volumes for his toughness and tenacity. His trusty camera equipment was with him on the trip. By now he had cut the weight of it down by less than half of the original twenty-five kilograms he had carried on his earlier expeditions, which lightened the expedition's load considerably. But the weather was either wet or overcast and he took few photographs.

The difficulties were far from over at Scone Creek junction. 'There we had to do an elaborate sparring of the Creek before we could get over,' he told Newton. Sparring was the term for felling a tree and dropping it across a creek or river.[301]

Paul Powell, who travelled up the same valley some 15 years later, wrote in 1993:

> 'We had better weather than Ebenezer; and the track up to Scone Creek was more open. Though that 'most awful swamp' on the plateau between the Whataroa and the Perth junction and Harry Heveldt's little shack, was something of a miasma

300. Ibid.
301. Ibid.

sans alligators... The deer cullers' cage across the Perth was a Godsend - it made it possible for us to cross to the Great Unknown side.'[302]

Dr Teichelmann was clearly missing a guide of the calibre of Alec Graham or Jack Clarke. (He spells Clarke without an 'e') In a reference to Jack Lippe, his alpine guide, Teichelmann writes,

> 'A good chap, splendid porter and general Camp manager but oh so slow and unenterprising. Fortunately I had the good fortune to have Harry Butland with us, a splendid bushman, good cragsman, although no alpine experience, he saved the situation. He organised the bridge and did most of the track making, it was a bad river that we could not cross. Lippe was always getting lost in the bush and as he was a big man, he was slow in getting through it. I thought I would naturally be the weakling of the party, not being very young, but was surprised to find that I could carry a 35 to 40lb swag for 8 to 10 hours without being played out. The only pity of it was that I should be spending my energies in the bush instead of the snow regions.'[303]

Harry Butland was the one who saved the expedition from more difficulties. An ex-Klondyke miner and an expert bushman, Butland was from a well-known Whataroa family. His bush skills enabled the party to achieve a reasonable amount of success, and it took him a lot of hard physical work to do that. The sub-tropical forest with its prolific and luxuriant growth can make for tiring travelling and difficult navigating. Supplejack lianas wove impenetrable webs of tangle, precipitous bluffs forced long and grovely detours, slippery boulders jammed creek beds like a fog-induced snarl-up on a motorway, and always the damp and the wet. Never does the West Coast forest dry out. Boots are sucked down into the mire and snaking roots reach out to trip the unwary and tired. Harry was the man that knew how to deal with these problems.

After weeks of bad weather, Teichelmann pushed on up to the Main Divide from the camp at the Scone Junction. It took days of blazing, track cutting and reconnoitring to reach Sealey Pass and finally onto the Godley Glacier.

---

302. Paul Powell, personal correspondence. 26 June, 1993.
303. Letter to Newton, Teichelmann. 6 May 1924. Graham Collection, Hokitika.

'I have not a single photo of the high region there, the pass was reached in a fog and nothing could be seen thirty yards away. We then established a camp a day's march further up the Perth and from it we nearly reached a saddle into the Rangitata and the Adams branch of the Wanganui, but high snow drove us back, this was well into March. At the end of just on six weeks, bad weather made a return necessary.'[304]

Camps like this give some respite from the wet weather.

The return trip to Whataroa from Scone junction took only two days compared to the 14 days of track cutting on the way in. As ever, Teichelmann enjoyed the bush and commented to Newton that 'we went through some fine forest country and in many respects the trip was very interesting'. He had blazed a track up to Sealey Pass and to the

204. Ibid.

head of the Perth, which opened the valley up for later mountaineers. Will Kennedy comments of Teichelmann's attitude:

> Never once did he openly show signs of disappointment...He was cheerful throughout, joking as each heavier downpour struck the tent, and actually bursting out laughing whenever he caught a doleful expression on the face of and member...This attitude of his, together with his recitals of his experiences of the past under even more trying circumstances, simply made it impossible to be downcast for long in his company.

Others were to appreciate the pioneering work of Teichelmann.

Ten years later in 1934, a party of S. H. Barnett, B. R. Turner, W. M. E. Mirams, and D. V. Apperley verified the difficulty of the Scone Creek. The bridge that Butland had built in 1924 was five metres above Scone Creek. Since then the creek had risen five and a half metres and washed the bridge down to the sea, which forced the 1934 expedition to swim the creek on a rope.[305]

On New Year's Eve, 1939, Paul Powell, 'Bonk' Scotney and Jim Croxton recalled the efforts of the 1924 party.

> 'We had a memorable New Year's night at Scone Creek where the lightning flared and the thunder came rolling down from Sealey Pass. Close to the roaring water we found a cave with a sandy floor and drew lots who should first eat from an ancient can of bully beef. Was it a relic of Teichelmann's 1924 expedition to the Perth?
>
> "Tonight," said Bonk, stirring the meat into the evening stew, "We'll be eating alpine history."'[306]

Although Powell's party got a couple of fine days which permitted them to do the first ascent of The Great Unknown, they were plagued with the Perth's notorious weather that Teichelmann had written about. 'The Perth is one of those streams that runs nearly their whole course parallel with the Divide, and when it rains in Westland, of course we got it, and when it rained or was bad weather in Canterbury in came over enough to prevent high climbing'.

---

305. John Pascoe, *Unclimbed New Zealand*, Allen & Unwin. p123.
306. Paul Powell, *Just Where Do You Think You've Been?* A.H. & A.W. Reed, 1970. p56.

Paul Powell's final words in his chapter on the Perth were perhaps an epitaph to Teichelmann's last major alpine expedition:

'There was a purple haze over the inner cirque where we'd camped, and in noonday a drowsy stillness, a Xanadu atmosphere which made us forget why we'd come to climb. The mountains were very old and infinitely wiser than we: they had time, but ours was almost gone.

.... But I took the smoky taste of bush tea, the blood-red rata, the green forest, the mountains, and the nights of camps and friends with me to war. They were my citadel'.[307]

It was a different year and a different war but the headwaters of the Perth, the Wanganui, the Rakaia are the citadel of Teichelmann. Here he carried out the dying wishes of his mentor G. J. Roberts, of his friend Charlie Douglas, and made a last ditch effort to connect up with the Wanganui trip he made in 1911.[308]

Although the last big trip was over, his name pops up in the first Defiance Hut book on 14 June, 1924.[309] The entry simply reads,

June 14th	Mona Wilson	Featherston
	P. Graham	Waiho
	E. Teichelmann	Hoka

Mona Wilson, nee Moore, was brought up in Carterton and married a dentist, Ivor Wilson, who served on the West Coast as a locum dentist in the latter part of the First World War. Mary, their first child was born in Dr Teichelmann's house and was her Godfather. It was Teichelmann, known to the Wilson's as 'Dr. Ebbie' who introduced Mona to the mountains. According to her daughter Mary, Mona used to take an annual holiday separate from her family and would leave the children with grandparents. Once in Hokitika, she would stay with Teichelmann, and he would drive her down to Franz Josef

Encouraged by the Doctor, Mona Wilson went on to do some excellent climbing in the years ahead with ascents of prominent peaks and passes, including Malte Brun and Mount Spencer.[310]

---

307. Ibid.
308. Teichelmann, Letter to Newton. op cit.
309. Defiance Hut Book 1912- 1930. Graham Collection, Hokitika.
310. Langton, Graham, letter dated 26 May 1994. Other information from Guide Aspiring, Frank Alack. Oswald-Sealy

Retirement:

Two-and-a-half years after Ebenezer Teichelmann completed his last major expedition into the mountains, he retired from the permanent position of Medical Superintendent, Westland Hospital on 31 August 1926, after 30 years of service. He was 68 years of age. A farewell held at the Town Hall on that day was well attended by heads of local bodies and a large gathering of friends and townspeople. It was reported fully in The Hokitika Guardian. They published the full contents of eight speeches together with two telegrams from West Coast politicians expressing their regret at being unable to attend.

The Mayor said they had been called together to say farewell to the Doctor who was leaving on Thursday on an extended trip to America and Europe. The Doctor had been with us now for many years and was well-known to every household from Taramakau to Jackson's Bay. The Doctor would be welcomed to any house in Westland... Mrs. W. Wilson said she was sorry Mr Wilson could not be present. She recalled Dr Teichelmann's arrival some years ago. She was very young then (laughter). Dr Teichelmann was an outstanding professional man, but he served the people in many ways in other spheres. He was a citizen of renown, a director of several local institutions, a sportsman, and a friend of all. Dr Teichelmann was always cheery and it was pleasing to see him about town day by day. Mrs Wilson expressed the concern felt for the Doctor's welfare when on one occasion through stress of weather he had overstayed his holiday time in the mountains, and the relief felt when he returned safe but tired. Mrs Wilson spoke tenderly also of the Doctor's concern for patients' welfare in critical times, and his desire to do all he could, no matter his own personal convenience.[311]

311. West Coast Historical Museum, Teichelmann file

Six other speakers spoke with obvious love, affection and appreciation for a man who had done so much for Hokitika and Westland. Then, it was the Doctor's turn to reply:

On rising to reply, Dr Teichelmann was received with loud applause. He said that looking around made him feel like old times. There were so many familiar faces present, friends whose presence brought back memories of twenty or thirty years ago. He came here a complete stranger. They had all been very kind and had adopted him as a son of Westland. He wanted to show his loyalty to his foster parents, and what he had done had been a pleasurable duty. If all cooperated in the right spirit the district would go ahead. For their kind wishes and the cordial expressions he desired to thank most heartily, as also for the useful gift from the citizens. (Loud applause). The singing 'For He's a Jolly Good Fellow,' and cheers for Dr Teichelmann concluded the proceedings.[312]

Four days after his retirement, Dr Teichelmann traveled overseas to Europe and America. In 1921 he had been elected to the position of Trustee of the Hokitika Savings Bank, and on this trip he had been selected to represent the Combined Trustee Savings Banks of New Zealand at a World Congress at Philadelphia in the USA.[313]

Once in Philadelphia, the Doctor found the conference 'a very important and busy one'. What impressed him most was the emphasis put on publicizing and promoting thrift and the methods used to attract the attention of the public to the advantages of saving money. There were several sessions at the conference and numerous committee meetings that he attended.

Returning to Hokitika in early March 1927, the Doctor was in time to be at the opening of the new Hokitika Savings Bank, a fine brick building in Hamilton Street. At the opening ceremony, the Hon. H. L. Michel, President of the Hokitika Savings Bank, welcomed Dr Teichelmann back to Hokitika and thanked him 'for the trouble and expense he had gone to, and for the able manner he had represented the Dominion institutions'.[312]

Retirement meant more time for conservation work especially with the Arthurs Park National Park, Lake Kaniere Scenic Reserve and his involvement in getting Reserve

312. Ibid.
313. Ibid.

status for a number of areas high in beauty and biodiversity, that had given him so much pleasure as a younger man. He encouraged a fledgling tourist industry and still contributed to the work of the New Zealand Alpine Club.

Lake Mahinapua later got reserve status and logging was prohibited thanks to Dr. Teichelmanns efforts

Teichelmann continued to make numerous trips into the lower mountain regions through until the early 1930s, although few of his trips were recorded. The evidence lies in his photographic collection scattered through the South Island of New Zealand. He also became increasingly involved in seeing that places of natural beauty which were home to much special flora and fauna were given some measure of protection.

In January 1925 an 18 year old lad, Charlie Carrington, wrote a letter to the Press under the pen-name of Cora Lynn 'expounding the beauties and grandeur of the headwaters of the Waimakariri and expressing surprise that such a place, within a few hours' journey of a city, should be so neglected'. Soon others rose to his support, including C. J. Thornton nd B. Wyn-Irwin, so that by Easter that year, he was guiding officials from the Government Tourist Department and the Canterbury Progress League up towards the Harman and Whitehorn Passes and the sources of the White and Waimakariri Rivers. As a result of his trip and subsequent meetings in Christchurch, the Christchurch Tramping Club was ormed, later to be renamed the Canterbury Mountaineering Club. Ebenezer Teichelmann was given the role of one of five vice-presidents, along with illustrious company of Arthur

14. Hokitika Guardian, 16 March, 1927.

D. Dobson, Guy E. Mannering, Professor Speight and W. A. Kennedy. President was C. S McCully, with Charlie Carrington as secretary-treasurer.[315]

His niece from Australia came to stay with him and climbed Alec Knob and looked along the ridge to Ebenezer Peak, named after her uncle.

Mountaineering still held great interes for the Doctor and his involvement in th New Zealand Alpine Club increased. A lecture entitled 'Mountaineering Pionee Climbers' was advertised in the Hokitik Guardian on 3 October, 1930. The lectur was given by Mr Arthur P. Harper and D E. Teichelmann, using 'slides on lantern'.[316]

In 1936-37 he became President of th New Zealand Alpine Club and als President of its Canterbury-Westlan Section from 1936-38.

An excerpt from the 1937 New Alpin Journal shows that at the age of 77 , h was still very active in promoting th beloved mountains of the West Coast.

The Annual Dinner, which was hel on 16th May, 1936, in conjunction wit the Annual Meeting of the Club, was a unqualified success, and probably the mo successful function yet organized by t Section. We were fortunate to preva upon the President, Dr. E. Teichelmann, to patronize the Dinner and entertain us wit an illustrated address. The attractive personality of Dr. Teichelmann and inimitab charm of his description of his early climbs and explorations in the West Coast mountai

315. Jack's Hut, op.cit.
316. Hokitika Guardian, 3 October, 1930.

made this Dinner a memorable event. The arrangements made by the special committee were fully appreciated by members, and the large attendance of 60 members and guests ensued its success.[317]

The importance of tourism to the economy of the Westland had long been recognized by the Doctor since early in the century. His time spent in the Swiss Alps in 1912 had shown him that whole communities could derive a sustainable livelihood from tourism. This fired him up even more to become a tourism advocate, a role that he doggedly carried out during the 1920s and 1930s. The Hokitika Borough Council had listened with interest to Teichelmann's frequent presentations on the tourist potential of Westland and contributed to the formation of a Tourist Development Committee in May 1935 by appointing the Doctor as its representative to a meeting of West Coast local bodies.

The thriving tourism attractions in Hokitika today can be attributed partly to his determination to see the area flourish on its natural resources, but in a sustainable way.

He continued playing tennis well into his seventies and kept his involvement in medicine by doing part-time work as an anesthetist at the Westland District Hospital after his retirement as Superintendent in 1926.[318]

Tennis was important part of Teichelmann's social life. It was through tennis that he developed a firm friendship with a number of women, including Flo Lewis. The Doctor held numerous positions in the Hokitika Tennis Club, including Patron and President. Both the Doctor and Flo Lewis were popular on the Hokitika social scene in the 20s and 30s and tennis was a very social activity.[319]

Tennis was played at the Methodist Church courts until the mid 1930s. Each year the West Coast Championships were played at either Hokitika or Greymouth with clubs from Westport, Greymouth and Hokitika competing. After the championships would be a major social function, which was a social highlight of the year. When the championships were held in Hokitika, the after-match social would often be held at Lake Kaniere, similar to a modern-day barbecue.[320]

---

317. NZAJ vol VII. JUNE 1937 No 24 p 173
318. Elsie Davidson, personal conversation. June 1993.
319. Henry Pierson, op cit.
320. Nell Stevenson and Hazel Kelly, personal conversation.

Two other keen members of the Hokitika Tennis Club, Nell Stevenson and Hazel Kelly (nee Keller) recalled the 1920s and early 30s when tennis was very popular and a great social sport. Nell Stevenson played tennis at high school and remembers playing doubles with Dr Teichelmann.

"He was very well known, and at first I felt intimidated by him. He loved to be up at the net and he would smash the ball to the right, left or centre. If he missed it he would say in a high voice, 'heet it Nell, heet it Nell.' "

Both Hazel and Nell remember the Doctor still playing tennis in 1929, when he would have been 70. Despite his age, he was fit and agile, and his wiry body and sharp mind and reflexes still made a formidable opponent. He never wore whites when playing tennis, only his trademark knickerbockers.[321]

Hazel Kelly recalls Flo Lewis quite clearly from her tennis days:

"One day we were at tennis and she was playing and she was rather big in the bus and she didn't wear a bra, and somebody said, 'Isn't it uncomfortable?' She said 'Oh no I just let them flop.' "[322]

The doubles team of Teichelmann and Lewis, Ebenezer in his knickerbockers and Flo playing bra-less, must have been quite a sight.

Another friend of the Doctor was Mrs Jane Butler, known to some as Madam Butterfly. Her husband, Bill, was a well-known sawmiller who managed mills at Ruatapu Bruce Bay and other parts of New Zealand. He died at a young age. The Doctor used to visit Madam Butterfly quite regularly. Mrs Butler was also a very social person and was great supporter of recreation. Ces Preston remembers taking banjo lessons from Mr Butler when he was young. When she died she left money for recreation purposes to b used by the Hokitika Borough Council.[323]

Teichelmann had a friendly relationship with a number of women, but none wer

---

321. Ibid.
322. Hazel Kelly, personal conversation.
323. Henry Pierson and Ces Preston, personal conversation.

Teichelemann with his car in the early 1930's

more dedicated to assisting him than were his housekeeper Miss Margaret Tomlinson, and Bess Hudson, his nurse in his private practice for many years. Margaret Tomlinson lived in the house next door to the Doctor, which he built for her.[324] She was an English woman and after Teichelmann died relatives of his came from Australia and met her to learn more of their Uncle Ebe.[325] To a publican's son at Woodstock in the early 1930s, ten miles outside of Hokitika, young Jim Keenan knew Bess Hudson by three words, Dr Teichelmann's nurse. "She was totally dedicated to the Doctor, never married and was always available to assist in time of need," recalled Jim Keenan.[326]

Not all were appreciative of their contacts with the Doctor however. A young 16 year old in 1932, former Mayor of Hokitika Henry Pierson, recalled an unplanned meeting with Teichelmann from the top of an apple tree in the dark:

---

324. Hazel Kelly, op cit.
325. Dorothy Fletcher, personal conversation.
326. Jim Keenan, personal conversation.

"Dr Teichelmann was quite friendly with Flo Lewis, and was visiting her at her home in Brittan Street when we raided her orchard. I was with Jack West, Lloyd Parry and Rupert Roberts when Teichelmann spied us from the window. He came out and with a squeaky voice and shouted, 'Come down you rascals, come down you scallywags,' as he prodded us with a long stick. Fortunately we managed to escape." [327]

Teichelmann with staff at the Graham Hotel Waiho. His niece on the far right.

327. Henry Pierson, personal conversation.

Teichelmann opening new wing at Seaview Hospital

Although young Henry and his friends had great respect for the Doctor, who was now in his seventies, typical of young people they had created another name for him. He was known as 'Dr Tickelbum'. [328]

It is easy to see this revered gentleman being the butt of many sniggers and jokes from youngsters who were insensitive to the protocol of society. He was an amusing sight to some as he pedaled his large black bicycle along the streets of Hokitika, wearing his plus four or knickerbocker trousers and Norfolk jacket, sporting a pointed goatee beard and bearing an odd German-sounding name.[329]

During his retirement years Dr Teichelmann continued to live in Hampden Street, and his house still stands there today.

328. Ibid.
329. Elsie Davidson, op cit.

The Doctor with Ethel Richardson a very accomplished artist who lived her latter years at Franz Josef Glacier.

1934 Newton Returns

What has been described by numerous historians as the greatest ever climbing trio in the history of New Zealand's mountaineering - Alec Graham, Canon H. E. Newton and Dr Teichelmann - got together again in 1934 and 1935. Canon Newton returned to New Zealand for a holiday in October 1934, and shipped with him his old Morris 14. Soon after his arrival in New Zealand he 'motored over the Otira' to see his aging comrade. According to Alec Graham, 'he was still full of booming enthusiasm'.[330]

The Doctor was greatly moved by Newton's visit, for their friendship was one that was forged under adversity in the period 1901-1907. Since then they had met in England during the First World War, and had corresponded regularly. Newton's visit also brought great joy to Alec and Peter Graham.

Teichelmann was now 75, and Newton in his early sixties. On his arrival in Hokitika, Newton spent some days staying with the Doctor.[331] However the 'some days' that Alec Graham refers to could have possibly been two or three weeks, judging by entries in Newton's diary. It is not hard to picture the two aging climbers reminiscing, poring over photographs, books, trips to Lake Kaniere and discussing Newton's planned trip with Alec Graham. Some years later Newton wrote that Teichelmann at the time 'was suffering from an obscure trouble of the jaw, but he had aged little in appearance, and was interested as ever in Alpine matters'.[332]

---

330. Alec Graham & Jim Wilson. op.cit.
331. Ibid.
332. NZAJ, 1939. p117.

Hokitika and Westland had changed a great deal since Newton's departure in 1907. His diary is laced with acute observations and makes great reading:

'I stayed with Dr Teichelmann in Hokitika and looked up a number of old friends. The thing that struck me most was the extraordinary difference in the look of the farms. When I had left nearly thirty years before the district had just been opened up and everything was pretty rough. Where land had been cleared many of the old tree stumps were still lying about and though there was plenty of feed, it was all rough grazing and the cattle just cows. Now the paddocks were obviously first class pasture and the cattle showed a large Jersey strain; comfortable homes were everywhere and decent sheds. I asked one man what he put it down to as there was obviously more than hard work and the answer was "the motor lorry". In the old days before the Otira tunnel, fertilizers were not only too expensive, but when the only transport from the railway was a spring cart for about sixteen miles with a river to ford, the necessary household stores took up most of the room. Now a motor will make several journeys in the day and bring up a big load. When I got further south it was almost more noticeable. Farmers who before had to drive sheep eighty miles to a fortnightly market in Hokitika and ford several big rivers, even if they did miss market through a flooded river, had only travel-worn animals to sell in a market that served but a small population. Now their sons were loading lambs in double-decker lorries in the afternoon which drove them up to Hokitika (or Ross) where they were put on a train and sold next morning at the great Addington Yards and freezing works near Christchurch on the other side of the island.'[333]

Canon Newton headed south to Graham's Hotel at Waiho on 13 December 1934 for about three-and-a-half months. From there he went off on numerous climbing forays. Unfortunately the Doctor's age precluded him joining his old friends Alec Graham and Canon Newton on the climbing trips, but he did make a number of trips to Waiho during Newton's long stay there, and they had many pleasant days together. Newton's first trip on his return to Waiho was a repeat of the first alpine expedition he did with Teichelmann in 1902 from Waiho over Graham Saddle to the Hermitage, returning by Baker Saddle to the Copland valley. His next trip was up the Fox Glacier:

333. Newton Diaries.

Canon Newton, Peter Grahan (standing) Ebenezer Teichelmann, and Alec Graham

'We made an attempt on Torres which failed partly owing to bad weather, but I found that I could not go the pace that was necessary and I gave up on an attempt on Mount Tasman over Mount Lendenfeld because I knew I could not go fast enough'.

There followed two further trips, one an unsuccessful attempt on Mount Elie de Beaumont by way of the Callery, and another by aircraft into the upper Arawhata with Alec Graham, Jack Cox, Louie Roberts, and Marion Scott, where they did the first ascent of Mount Eros.[334]

When Mary Louise Roberts died, her climbing partner Marion Scott wrote an

334. Alec Graham & Jim Wilson/ Newton Diaries.

Last known photo taken of Dr. Teichelmann

obituary that tells of the meetings between her, Alec Graham, Canon Newton and Dr Teichelmann:

'I have grateful memories of camps in the Arawata with Alex Graham and his old friend Canon Newton, of the long trek up the Cook, of many camps and picnics around the Franz Josef Glacier, rock-climbing on the boulders at Okarito Beach and a camp on Alec's Knob before climbing Ebenezer (Teichelmann), the two knobs that combine the two friends in characteristically modest fashion. There were the placid evenings round the log fires in the Graham household with Canon Newton, Dr Teichelmann and many other good friends, sometimes the little Doctor rounding on his companion of many climbs: "Now I'll tell one about Alex." I think these things were of as much value to Louie as her major climbs.'[335]

Dr Ebenezer Teichelmann died at the Westland Hospital on 20 December 1938, of a cerebral haemorrhage following a cerebral thrombosis ten days earlier. Two days later he was buried at the Hokitika Cemetery. A service was held for him in the All Saints Anglican Church. At the graveside, Father J. Finerty, Roman Catholic priest, conducted the ceremony. This final gesture of having an Anglican Church service and a Catholic Father conducting the graveside rites for a man who professed by faith to be a rationalist, showed that there is hope for unity in this world. His whole life had been devoted to healing and discovery.[336]

It was a poignant moment.

"O leave my bones at the Hokitika cemetery when I die," he had said some years earlier, when questioned about his future,[337] and being a lover of Stevenson's poetry, it was indeed "here he lies where he longs to be."

The Patriach had found his rest. He was in the forefront of applying scientific and medical knowledge as it became available, a voyage of discovery in surgery, medicine, rainforests, conservation and exploration. And on photographic plates he left his record.

Buried alongside his wife Mary, his gravesite is not far from the Westland Hospital where he gave over 30 years of medical service to the district, and in the distance Mount

335. NZAJ, 1969.
336. West Coast Times, death sighting.
337. West Coast Historical Museum.

Cook, Mount Torres, Mount Douglas, Glacier Peak, La Perouse - all peaks he climbed - dot the horizon. Not far away are the graves of his mates, of a kindred spirit; Charlie Douglas, G. J. Roberts, Dr. MacAndrew and Duncan Mcfarlane.

The graves of Mary and Ebenezer Teichelmann overlooking the Southern Alps of New Zealand.

Even the day after he died, Teichelmann's generosity was still being felt. Mrs K. Lee (nee Warren) was working in the Post Office Exchange and she said that "Teichie always gave Five Pound each year towards Post Office Christmas Cheer. This year Teichie died before Christmas, but before he died he had written out a cheque for Five Pounds, and the Post Office received the cheque the day after he died."[338]

Mount Teichelmann, Teichelmann Rock, Teichelmann's Corner, Teichelmann's Track, Teichelmann's Creek, Ebenezer Peak and Teichelmann's (Bed and Breakfast) guesthouse celebrate his memory.

Peter Graham recognized something many others were to verbalize in different ways. "I was drawn to the quaint little man," he said. Others described it as an attraction, a charisma, or a magnetic personality.

'He had that rare gift of always seeing the very best in his friends, for he especially loved and had much consideration for younger people, and I always felt he loved us in spite of our faults; yet; withal, he was so amazingly modest about his own gifts and especially concerning his mountaineering achievements,' wrote another friend in the Alpine Club Journal.

A small man, without an ounce of flesh, his physical powers were amazing. I can

338. Ibid.

still see him - slipping through the tangled bush like a Maori Hen and perfectly happy, while I panted and struggled behind in the vilest of tempers - and an enormous 'swag', above which the crown of a hat was just visible and below, the lower part of a pair of very thin legs.

... A fine character, a delightful companion, and one who, when climbing was almost dead in New Zealand, did so much by his climbs and his photographs to rekindle that enthusiasm for the hills which is bearing such good fruit among the new generation of climbers in the Southern Alps.'[339]

Andy Denis writing on one of the world's richest conservation areas, teeming with biodiversity and wonder, Te Wahipounamu, South-West New Zealand, spoke of those great conservation pioneers such as Teichelmann "... a celebration of the wisdom and foresight of those New Zealanders, who, from as early as the 1880s, have been aware of the necessity of setting aside large areas of unspoilt wild country both to protect their intrinsic values and for the benefit, use and enjoyment of those who need such places for inspiration, solitude and escape."[340]

The enduring glory of the land and mountains of South Westland are indeed a fitting tribute to this extraordinary man.

---

339. NZAJ, 1939

340. Craig Potton Publishing, *Te Washipounamu-South-West New Zealand World Heritage Area*-Photographs by Andris Apse, Introduction by Andy Dennis. 1997.

Acknowledgements

The smell of dubbin and smelly socks fills my nostrils when I think of Fox Glacier township, formerly Weheka, and Mike Browne, a permanent fixture there for a fair part of two millenniums. I remember in 1973 in Mary Kerr's guiding hut surrounded by hundreds of hobnail boots, drinking a beer as we cleaned boots. "You know Bob, Teichy, Alec and Peter Graham could cut steps all the way to the top of Cook, without crampons, using hobnail boots like this," Mike said showing me boots that were almost identical to those of Teichelmann. And at the bar after cleaning boots was former guide Mick Sullivan, who, after a few gins, would argue about the modern climber not being able to cut steps and referred to the golden era of Teichelmann and Newton. "I was operated on him by him on the kitchen table," said Mick rather matter of factly. In the 70s and early 80s when staying with Mike, characters like Oscar Coberger, Jack Cox, Franz Barta, who knew Teichelmann, would yarn to us about the wee Doctor, often over a wee dram.

In the early 1990s when seriously getting into this book, I met characters, characters larger than life, who knew Teichelmann personally, from Kevin and Des Nolan and Kerry Eggeling at Haast, Jack Bannister at Bruce Bay, Mick Sullivan at Fox Glacier, the Grahams and McCormacks at Franz and Okarito, to leaning on the bar at the Red Lion pub in Hokitika with stalwarts like Jim Keenan and Henry Pierson, and on Friday at the RSA with the above plus Kelly Wilson, Dick and Colin Thomas. Other memories which spring to mind are the animated conversations in the homes of Hec and Elsie Davidson, Ces Preston, often over roaring wood fires, tea and scones, and the entertaining stories told by Nell Stevenson, Hazel Kelly, Ellen Chesterman who knew Teichy well and were able to give superb cameos of the tennis, women he was close to, social habits, and who talked to me about his emotional and sensitive qualities.

This book could not have been written without the inspiration and full support of Dorothy Fletcher, daughter of Alec Graham, who gave me free access to her archives (The Graham Collection) and provided weeks and weeks of her time. She read all the early manuscripts and made so many helpful suggestions. Gar Graham, the son of Peter Graham, also was very helpful in providing vivid first-hand impressions.

My interviews with the late Hec Davidson were invaluable. Hec was 90 when I interviewed him in 1992 and he knew Dr Teichelmann and his milieu very well and provided a real insight into the man as did Elsie Davidson, (nee Cameron) his wife, who worked with Teichelmann as a nurse.

Dorothy Fletcher, daughter of Alec Graham, who knew Teichelmann as a girl, with Bob McKerrow

Sadly Hec died the following year.

I got some very interesting information from Jane Ward's grandson, Tom Ward, whose grandmother looked after Explorer Charlie Douglas and this helped me understand the relationship between Douglas, Roberts and Teichelmann much better,

Trish McCormack shared a number of articles and publications she had compiled over the years, and through her research, had her own perspective on Teichelmann. Special thanks to her father and mother, Peter and Elizabeth, who helped me a lot when I lived at Franz Josef, and Peter in particular who brought Teichelmann out of pages of history into the realm of reality. Special thanks to Ray Hooker, Ted Brennan, Anne Hutchison, Jim Russell, Hemi Te Rakau, Bruce Watson, Mike Browne, Paul Madgwick, Hugh Logan, Dave Bamford, John Nankervis, Hugh Wilson, Hugh Logan, Trish McCormack, Trevor Chinn and Ed Cotter who gave feedback on earlier drafts.

Paul Powell was great; testy, warm, sometimes cynical, when he came to stay with me at Franz Josef and talk about Teichy's era, which he partially overlapped with.

To the late Vern Leader with whom I did a Grand Traverse of Mount Cook when he was 64, I owe special thanks to him for firing me up about Teichelmann as early as 1971, and for his interest and detailed feedback on an earlier draft.

Anne Hutchison gave of her time freely to assist me research the early history of Hokitika and Westland.

Special thanks to Bruce White, New Zealand Alpine Journal Editor from 1996 to 2002, who spent considerable time editing the book and crafting it from that of an enthusiastic amateur to a more readable version. And to Angela his wife, who went for a long time with little help in the garden and in renovating the house. Later, John Tulloch, gave it a final polish in New Delhi on the strength his grandfather was a doctor in Hokitika in the 1930's and knew Teichy.

I am especially grateful to the Canterbury Mountaineering Club who so kindly made photographs available from the Teichelmann, photo collection. I am most greatful, to the New Zealand Alpine Club for its support, especially Ross Cullen and Dave Bamford.

Colin and Betty Monteath were a tower of strength in providing support & inspiration. Colin was able to locate the Teichelmann photo album from which many photos illustrate this book.

Also to Bruce Watson for his encouragement when times were rough and for all his help.

The Birchfied family at Ross provided fun, food & shelter when I did the final rewrite of the book.

And finally, just as the manuscript was almost complete, I met Simon Nathan in Delhi, who works for the Institute of Geological Sciences and at the Stout Research Centre, Victoria University, New Zealand, who spent over 20 years on the West Coast as a Geologist, and gave valuable feedback on the final draft.

Sadly, many of the people I mention here, are no more.

To my children, Anita, Tania, Ruia, Kira, Aroha, Ablai and Mahdi, thanks for putting up with a Dad glued to a computer or yarning to people of yesteryear when I should have been out playing, or talking with you.

PHOTO CREDITS:

The majority of photographs have been taken by Dr. Ebenezer Teichelmann, generously made available by the Canterbury Mountaineering Club, Teichelmann Photo Collection. **Other photographs have been kindly made available by.**

	Pages
Adams, Grace*	83,84
Birchfield, Paul	41
Hokitika Borough Council	13,14,32,33,62,66,67,70,94
Hokitika Historical Museum	61
Fletcher, Dorothy/ Graham Collection,Hokitika	28,51,64,72,92,94,109,179,196,234,237,239,240,244
McKerrow, Bob	12,85,119,126,160,168,174,181,215
McKerrow, Kira	250
Thomas, Colin and Dick	45,49,50
Tomlinson, C.A.	54
White, Bruce	246

*Grace Adam's gave approval to reproduce photographs of Oscar and Dagmar Coberger from her book, Jack's Hut

Dorothy Fletcher and Jim Wilson gave approval to use photographs and maps from their book *Uncle Alec and the Grahams of Franz Josef*, and Hugh Wilson gave approval to reproduce the maps drawn by him.

LIST OF ASCENTS AND EXPLORATION

SEASON	ASCENT	DATE	PARTY	COMMENTS
1899	Spencer and Burton Glaciers	Nov or Dec 1899	A.Woodham, C. Stoner & P. Graham	1st recorded trip on these 2 glaciers
1900	Craig Peak, Mts.Gaskill, Purity, McIntosh, Ferguson and Vickers	January		1st traverse of Victoria range & 1st ascent all peaks
1902	Graham Saddle via Goat Path	31.01.02	Batson, Newton	1st west to east from Waiho to Hermitage
	Baker Saddle	6.02.02	Above party plus J. Clarke	1st crossing
	Strauchon Glacier	7.02.02	above	1st party to descend glacier
1903	Chancellor Dome	Jan. 1903		1st ascent
	Engineer Col	"	Newton, P.Graham	1st ascent
	Pioneer Pass	"		1st ascent
	Fox Glacier	"		1st party to explore upperr reaches
1904	Mt. Ollivier	Jan 1903	P.Graham	
	Glacier Dome	7.3.02	P.Graham, J.Clarke	
	Pioneer Pass	8.2.02		1st crossing E to W.
1905	La Perouse Glacier			
	Harper Saddle	29.01.05	Newton, A. Graham Low	1st crossing
	Glacier Dome	2.02.05		
	Mt Cook/Aoraki	2.02.05	Newton, Low, A. Graham, Clarke	3rd ascent
	Copland Pass		Newton, A. Graham	

SEASON	ASCENT	DATE	PARTY	COMMENTS
1906	La Perouse	1.02.06	Newton, Low, A.Graham	1st ascent
	Col. on Balfour Range			Some speculation as to whether they climbed Vanguard or possibly Belmont
1907	Mt. Halcombe	26.01.07	Newton, A.Graham	1st ascent
	Glacier Peak	27.01.07		1st ascent
	Mt. Douglas	28.01.07		1st ascent
	Mt. Torres	04.02.07		1st ascent
	Pioneer Psss	07.02.07		1st west to east crossing
	Mt. Moltke	Late 1907	Rev Kemp, A.Graham.	1st ascent
	Mt.Roon	"		1st ascent
	Mt.Anderegg	"		1st ascent
	Mt. Bismark	"		1st ascent
1908	Glacier Dome (Waiatoto)		A.Graham,D.Nolan	1st ascent
1909	Graham Saddle		A.Graham	
	Mt. Green	15.02.09	Dr.Vollman, A.Graham. P.Graham	1st ascent
	Mt. Walter	15.02.09	"	1st ascent
	Copland Pass		A.Graham	
1910	Mt. Chudleigh	19.2.10	A.Graham, P.Graham	1st ascents of low and middle peaks
	Mein's Knob		A.Graham	
	Ramsay Glacier			
	Whitcome Pass			

SEASON	ASCENT	DATE	PARTY	COMMENTS
1911	Lambert Glacier		A.Graham, J. Clarke	
	Mt.Soddart	01.02.11		1st ascent
	Snowy Peak			1st ascent
	Mt. Tyndall			1st ascent
	Malcolm Peak			1st ascent
	Clarke Saddle			(between Lord and Ramsay Glaciers)
1912	Footstool	03.04.12		
	SWITZERLAND			
	Wellenkuppe			Possibly with members of the Alpine Club.
	Furgengrat			
	Theodal Pass			
1914	Mt. Spencer	Feb 1914	A. Graham	1st ascent
1924	**Glacier region**	23.02.24	Capt. Buckley & Havelock Williams	1st flight over the South Westland Glaciers
	Sealey Pass	March 1924		

26 first ascents of mountains. Seven first ascents or crossings of passes, cols or saddles.

Glossary - Mountaineering/terms

Abseil — A means by which a rope can be descended safely, the speed of descent being controlled by friction that can be produced by wrapping the ropes round the body or by using an abseil device.

Adze — The wider cutting edge on the head of an ice axe.

Arete — A narrow ridge of rock, ice or snow.

Avalanche — The rapid downwards movement of a mass of snow or perhaps ice.

Bergschrund — The last big crevasse at the head of a glacier. It can often form a formidable barrier at the start of a route as the upper lip is often much higher than the lower one.

Sometimes referred to as a schrund

Bivouac or bivvy — To bivouac (or bivvy or bivi) is to spend the night in the open on a route of a mountain.

Cairn — A man-made pile of rocks to mark a route. Helpful for navigation.

Cirque — At the head of a glacier where the snow parts from the rock. Often semi circular

Col — A small pass between two peaks

Couloir — A steep gulley or gorge frequently filled with snow or ice-filled

Cornice — An overhanging edge of snow on a ridge.

Gendarme — A pinnacle or isolated rock tower frequently encountered along a ridge

Glissade — A usually voluntary act of sliding down a steep slope of snow. Usually an ice axe or pole is used to lean on while the feet act like skiis.

Moraine — Piles of debris carried down and deposited by a glacier. These ridges of stones, earth and rubble can be in three main forms; terminal moraine is found at the glacier snout, lateral moraine being along the sides and medial moraine where two glaciers meet.

Névé	Permanent snow lying at the head of a glacier. Often refers to permanent granular ice formed by repeated freeze-thaw cycles.
Saddle	A high pass between two peaks, larger than a col.
Stastrugi	Furrowed ice shaped by wind from a prevailing direction..

Glossary - New Zealand words

Bushbashing	Moving through dense bush
Billy	Billy can. A pot without a handle.
Dubbin	A waterproof solution for boots.
Haangi	A Maori cooking pit where food is cooked over pre-heated rocks
Kea	A curious indigenous bird
Kiwi	A flightless, nocturnal ground bird.
Maori	Indigenous people to New Zealand
Matai	Native tree -black pine
Miro	Native tree - brown pine
Meths	Methylated spirits (slang)
Pakehe	Swampy regions
Plunket	An institution supporting Mother and Babies. Named after the founder, Lord Plunket
Rimu	Native tree - red pine
Slasher	A heavy large knife-like blade with a long wooden handle for slashing through bush.
Swag	A back pack
Swagged	Carrying a pack or a large bundle.
Swagging	Similar meaning to above
Weka	An indigenous flightless brown bird.

Index

Abattoirs and Slaughterman's Act 63
Aboriginal people of South Australia 18-20
Adams Gorge 207
Adams, Ruth 161
Addington yards 242
Adelaide 15, 20-23,25
Adelaide, Port 23, 25
Adelaide University 23
Afghanistan 2,
Agean Sea 43
Alec's Knob 191,245
Alexander the Great 44
Allen, James 42
Almer Hut 76
Almer Rock 221
Alpine, Lake 71
Altenberg 18
Amery, L.S. Rt. Hon. 74,76
Amery Dr. Rob 23
Anderegg, Mt. 180
Anderson, Charles 159
Aoraki Mt. Cook vii,1,65,**154,215**
Apperley, D.V. 229
Arahua Pa 56
Arahura Valley 36,38,53
Arawhata 243
Arrowsmith Mountains 93,202
Arthur's Pass 78,81,83,85,104,106,232
Arthur's Pass National Park 86,90
Ashburton 200
Aspiring, Mt. 187-190,195,197,219
  North Face 189
  Western Face 197
Auckland 76,221
Auckland Graphic 69
Australia 3,17,18,30
Australian Military Forces 25
Austria 3
  -Emperor of 78
Austrian Alpine Club 193
Avalanche Camp 118
Avro 504K 70,73
Ayres, Harry vii

Baird Range 116,166
Baker Saddle 127,132,133,242
Balfour Range 103,149,162
Balfour River 150,162
Ball Hut 130,132,142,143,153,157,178
Ball Pass 1
Bannister, Dave 47
Bannister, Jack 64,76
Bannister, George 65
Bannister, John William 30,64
Barnett, S.H. 229
Barron Canyon **201**
Bartholomew's Hospital 23
Batson's Hotel 210
Batson, W 129,130-134
Bealey Glacier 84
Belfast 23
Belgium 41
Bell, Dr. James Macintosh 168
Benighted Creek 203,
Berlin 17,40,214
Bettney, Mary 24

Bill the Maori 65,115
Birmingham 15, 23-25,41,214
Birmingham General Hospital 24
Birmingham Workhouse 23,24
Bismark, Mt. 180
Blackburn's Saddle 124
Blossom 56,57
Blue Lookout 93,203
Blue Spur 29
Bonatti, Walter 1
Bradey, Lydia 1
British War Office 42
Bristol Top, Mt. 179
Bowie Ridge 157
Brennan,Ted 171
Brown, Annie 36
Browne, Mike 125
Brunnerton 31
Bruce Bay 17, **32,** 47,64,76,95
Buckley, Maurice 70,72,73,75
Buhl, Hermann 1
Bulgarians 45
Burster Camp 118
Burster Range 116,219
Burton Glacier 4,118,125
Burton Valley 3
Butland, Harry 226,227
Butler, Guy 81
Butler, Jane, 236

Café de Paris 37
Callington 22
Callery 4,116,117,118,125,194
Callery Ridge 125
Cameron, Donald 96
Cameron, Elsie 38,39,40
Cameron, Elsie (daughter) 38,55
Cameron, John 38
Canada 80
Canadian 47
Canavan's Knob 219
Canopy Bluff 203
Canterbury 199,211,214,216,229
Canterbury Progress League 78,81,216
Canterbury Mountaineering Club 2,106,233
Canterbury Tramping Club 81
Carnegie Building 32
Carnegie Free Public Library 3,55,60,**61**
Carnegie, William 60
Carrington, Charlie 233,234
Cass Square 31
Castle Rock 150
Chambers. H. 211,222
Chancellor Dome 137
Chancellor Ridge 137,140,
Chesterman, Ellen, nee Cameron 96
Christchurch 3,69,81,106,107
Christchurch Press 213
Christchurch Public Library 111
Christchurch Tramping Club 111,233
Chudleigh, Mt. 199
Chung, Yhu 36
Clarke, Jack 132,140-142,145,153,155,
156,168,169,195,203,208,210,222,226,227
Clarke Saddle 151,153,161,
Coberger, Annelise 85
Coberger, Dagmar **84,**85
Coberger, Oscar **83,84,**85
Codford Depot 48,49
Cockayne, Leonard, Dr. 80,81,111,216
Collet, Mick 226
Cone Rock 174
Conservation, Dept. of 90
Conway Peak 179
Cook, Mt. 26,28,104,106,115,124,143,
149,151,156,159,164,185,**194,**219,220,246

Cook River/Valley 4,102,103,149,159,160,211,245
Copland Pass 140,157,195,199
Copland Valley 123,132,134,242
Cora Lynn 233
Cox, Jack, 243
Craig's Freehold 35
Craig Peak 123, 124
Croxton, Jim 229
Cum. Jimmy 67,**68,** 68,115

Dahme 17
Dale, Alf 108,**124,**125
Dampier, Mt. 115,164
Dan's Peak 93
Darby, S.C. 89
Davidson, Elsie 100
Davidson, Hec 180
Davidson, Malcolm 64
Defiance, Cape 103
Defiance Hut, 74,**74**,76,220,221,222
de la Beche Bivvy 11,130,167,**168**
de la Beche, Mount 11, 13,74
Denis, Andy 247
Dennistoun, James R 51,94,178,**179**,183, 195,202,206,220,225
Dickens, Dick 147
Diggers' hut 149,159
Dobson, Arthur D 83,234
Donne T.E. 140,216
Dorian 46
Dorothy Falls 87
Douglas, C.E. (Charlie) 30,63,65,91,**92**-101,123,149,184,186,187,188,204,230,246
Douglas, Mt. 140,146,173-175,246
Douglas Rock 134
Drummond Peak 116
Dresden 41,214
Dresden Lutheran Missionary Society 18
Dublin 15

Earle, Laurence 195,197
Ebenezer settlement 21
Ebenezer Peak 246
Edinburgh 15,60
Eggeling homestead 185
Egypt 3,47
Elie de Beaumont, Mount 26,113,116,118,**119,**181,185,195,243
Engineer Col. 144
England 2,3,17,22,30,48,179
English Alpine Club 2,68,151,212,213,216
English 193
Eros, Mt., 243
Estonian 68, 84
Evans, David John 76,89
Evans Creek 128
Everest, Mt., 112,215
Evolena 150

Ferguson, Mt. 124
Fitzgerald, Edward 65,124
Finerty, Father J., 245
Flanders 67
Fletcher, T.A 69
Fletcher, Dorothy 100,108,109,111,172,180,197
Fluerty, Joe 65
Footstool, Mt., 104,**143,**211
Ford, Mr. 67
Forks Hotel 147
Fox Glacier 63,69,103,104,**105,**112,211,242 123,137,146,171,184
Fox névé 137,145
Fox Range 123, 125
France 3,47
Francis Glacier 206

Franz Josef Glacier 3,70,71,**82,**103,112,124,199, 128,137,142,171,180,184,219,221,243
Freeman F.W, 83
French 18,45
Fritz (Kaiser)Range **110**,124,180,**181,**219
Furgengrat, Mt., 213
Fyfe,Tom 9-14

Gallipoli 46,67
Garden of Allah Snowfield 207
Garden of Eden Ice Plateau 208
Gaskill, Mt. 124
Gawler, George 18
Gething, Dr. 25
German 45,47
Germany 41,42,44
German Harry 115
Gibson Quay 16
Gill Memorial Prize 91
Gillespie's Beach **33**
Glacier Dome 143,145,153,178
Glacier Dome (Aspiring) 188
Glacier Peak 146,173
Goat Path 125, **126,**147,166,193
Godley Glacier 227
Golden Age Hotel 34,36
Gornergrat Hotel 2,212
Gornergrat ridge 2,4,212
Graham, Alec vii,28,42,49,63,65,86,100, 108,109,111,125,127,135,141,143-147,149-153, 155-157,167,171-180,199,200,215,219-223,225,241-245
Graham brothers 119,180, 185-189,193-195
Graham, Dave 74,**221**
Graham family 141
Graham, Louisa 109
Graham, Peter vii,3, 28,71,74,116,118,123, 125,134,135,138,183,193,197,202,215,223,225, 230,246
Graham's Hotel 242
Graham Saddle 74,123,127,129,147, 166,193,199,242
Grand Plateau 178
Great Unknown 227,229
Greece 3
Greek 18
Greek Army 45
Green, Mt. 194
Greville, Mr. (and survey party) 191
Greymouth 26,69,235
Grey Peak 139,142
Grey Valley 32,80
Grey, George Governor 21
Gulch Creek 159
Gulch Glacier 149

Haast 76
Haast, Mt. 139,142,177,179
Haast Ridge 104,143,144,151,178
Haidinger, Mt. 10, **11,**13,115,124,140
Halcombe, Mt. 103,173
Hall M.J. Mrs. 36
Hall, Rob 1
Hamburg 18
Hampden Street 32,115,155,172,239
Hamilton Street 32, 60,232
Hamner Jack 169
Han's Bay 86
Handorf 23
Hansell, Rev. 142
Happy Valley 20
Hargreaves, Alison 1
Harihari 56,128
Harper, A.P. 63,65,68,95,96,124,149,225,234
Harper, Rosamond 74
Harper Saddle 149,151,161
Harry the Whale 115

Hayes, Bully 16
Head, Capt. B 195,197
Hillary, Sir Edmund 161
Heveldt, Jack 147
Heveldt, Harry 226
Hende, Carl 56,203
Hende's Creek 203
Hende's Ford 56,128
Hende's Ferry 203,209
Hermitage 106,132,134,141,152,157,220
166,167,176,179,193,**194**,211,242
Hicks, Mt. 161,164,165
Hochstetter Dom 194
Hodgkins, William 11
Hokitika 3,12,13,15,17,24-27, 29, 30,31 ,35,
40, 51,5 2,5 4,61 ,63, 70, 73,74, 95, 110, 115,
141, 15,165,189,190,193,195,211,235,239,241
Hokitika Abattoir 61,**62,**63
Hokitika Borough Council 63,76,235,236
Hokitika Cemetery 245
Hokitika Exhibition 112
Hokitika Harbour Board 59,76
Hokitika Guardian 17,34
Hokitika River 16
Hokitika Savings Bank 60,74,232
Hokitika Tennis Club 235,236
Hokitika Wharf 16
Hokitika Wildfoods Festival 31
Holdfast Bay 18
Hooker Glacier/Valley 132,151
Hornchurch 48,49
Horo Koau 138
Hudson, Bess 35,237
Hudson, John, 35
Humphrey's Gully 54

Influenza Epidemic (1918) 51,52
Ingles, Dr. J.K. 69
International Conference of Savings Banks
74
International Exhibition (1907) 216
Ireland 3, 17

Jackson's Bay 17,33,76,184,185,231
Jaenicke Missionary Institute 18
Jaffray Suburban Hospital 24
Jane Douglas, S.S.75,171,184
Jefferies, W.J. 104
Jewish 45,53
John Pascoe Ridge 207
Jones' Flat 203
Julius, Bishop 127

Kaplan, Jonathan 38,39
Kaniere, Lake **79,** 86,87,90,95,99,104,241
Kaniere, Lake Scenic Reserve 78,86,87,90,232
Karangarua Valley 134
Karrawirraparri 20
Katies Col. 161,176
Kaurna 18-21,23
Kellers Hotel 32,67
Kelly, Hazel 98,236
Kelly, Mary 63
Kemp, Rev. 180
Kennan, Jim 237
Kennedy, Mark, Lt. 47
Kennedy, W.A.(Will) 33,63,103,106,108,
111,210,234
King, Dr, Truby 169
King, S. L. 220
Klose, Pastor S. 20
Kornergrat Ridge 4
Kowhitirangi 36,200

Lake Heron Station 200
Lambert Col 205
Lambert Glacier 202,203-206,208,210
Lambert Gorge 204

Lambert Icefall 204
Lambert Junction 93
Lambert, Mt., 104
Landsborough Valley 197
La Perouse Mt.151 181,246
La Perouse Glacier 103,149
Lee, Mr. 115
Lee, K. Mrs., 246
Lembet Camp, 45
Lendenfeld, Mt., 115,138,139,144,179
Lendenfeld Saddle 11
Leipzig 41,214
Lewis, Flo 235,236,238
Linda, Glacier 104,219,220
Lindon, L, 199
Lippe, Jack 211,227
Lithuania 53
Logan, Hugh 180
London 15,23 53
Longdon, Mr. 106
Longfellow, H.W 1.
Lord Range 104,203,205,206,210
Lord River 209
Louper River 200
Low R.S. 151,**156,** 159,161,164-170
Lyell Glacier 200,202,206

MacAndrew, Dr.Herbert 29,30,51,60,246
Macfarlane, Duncan 30,246
MacKay, W 83
Mackay Rocks 166,221
Mackintosh girls 134
Madgwick, Paul 63
Maheno N.Z.H:S. **50**
Mahinapua, Lake 71,73,90
Main Divide 31,205,227
Makawhio 65
Malcolm Glacier 208,209
Malcolm Peak 104,**206,208**
Malispina, Mt. 151
Malte Brun Hut 103,142,193,**196,**230
Malte Brun Range **196**,199
Mannering, G.E. 69
Maori 27,64,68,76
Maori Hen 247
Mapourika, Lake **26**,71 ,**222**
Marquette, H.M.T.S 43
Marshall, Prof. Pat 168
Marshall, Colin 189
Mason's Science College 23
Matterhorn 2,200,**212**,213,215,219
Matukituki Valley 195
Maximilian Ridge/Range 116
McAlpine,W.M 83
McCully 234
McDonald family 151
McIntosh, Mt. 124
Medical Superintendant 3, 14,17,231
Mediterranean Sea 47
Mein's Knob 200
Melbourne 25
Messner, Reinhold 1
Meyer, Pastor H, 20
Michel, H.L 61,232
Mikonui River 66
Minarets 11,13, 74,115,116
Miner's hut 149
Mirams, W.M.E. 229
Moltke, Mt. 71,180,191,**215**
Monteath, Colin 2,107
Morphett Vale 22
Morris 14

Nathan, Simon 95
Newton, Henry E. 49,69,106,108,123,125,127, **128**-130,132,**133**,137-152,55-157,159-165,171-180,186,199,207,221,226,228,241-245

Newton Peak 207
Newton Rocks 129
New Zealand 3,4,17,29,30,40,46,76,89,215, 241,106,107,181,247
New Zealand Alpine Club 68,74,76,100,183, 215, 223,233,234
Canterbury –Westland Section 69,234
New Zealand Alps 91
New Zealand Alpine Journal 69,104,150
New Zealand Army 42
New Zealand Expeditionary Forces 2.51
New Zealand (Christmas) Graphic 108,109
New Zealand Gazette 88
New Zealand Illustrated 196
New Zealand Stationary Hospital 43,45
Nicholson, Daniel 21
Nicholson, Margaret 21
Nicholson, Mt., 206
Nolan, Dennis (Din) 185
Nolan Homestead 37
Nolan, Matt 185

Omoeroa River 96
Okarito 17,36,72,147
Okarito Lagoon 71,73
Okarito River 71
Okuru 37,78,185
Ollivier Mt. 142
Osmers, Herman 171,172,176
Otira Tunnel 69,**70,**81,242
Otira Valley 81

Paparoa 31,90,106
Paringa 95
Pascoe, John 95,98,169
Paris 15
Park, George 100
Parry, Lloyd 238
Perth River 223,226,228,229
Perry, George 48,78.80,104
Philadelphia 74,232
Piersson, Henry 237,239
Piggery Charlie 115,
Piltawodli 20
Pioneer Pass 117,137,**139,14,** 177,179
Pioneer Ridge 103,146,171,172,223
Pinky's Flat 20
Porter, H.E.L. 191
Port Adelaide 23
Port Said 43,47,100
Potsdam 18
Powell, Paul 189,226,229,230
Preston's Bakery 39,40
Preston, Ces 55,65,98,99,236
Preston, Hugh Graham 39,40
Price's River **201**
Princess Theatre 17
Pukaki 168
Punakaiki 31,78,90,104,106
Purgatory Creek 141
Purity, Mt. 124

Queen's University 23

Rakaia River 198,199
Rainy Camp 116
Ramsay Glacier 93,200
Rangitata River 225,228
Clyde Branch 206
Rebuffat, Gaston, 1
Red Creek Farm 22,23
Red Cross 2
Red Lion Hotel 3,65
Reefton 53,54
Renton, P.H. 66
Renton, W.J. 66
Revell Street 15,17,34,62
Rhone Valley 150

Richardson, Ethel 240
Richmond, Jock 220
Riddiford, Earle 189
Rimu 71
Roberts, G.J. 30,60,63,86,91-**94,** 96-99,101,115,140,202,230
Roberts, Marie Louise 243,245
Roberts, Rupert, 238
Robinson, John Noble 89
Rohutu 12
Rolleston, Mt.84
Rona 16
Roon, Mt. 180
Rope Creek 129
Ross township 33,34,71,73,165,171
Ross, Malcolm 9-13,69,100,169
Ross, Forrest 10
Ross, Vicar 127
Ruatapu, 53
Rudolf Glacier 129,166,174
Royal Geographic Society 91

Sage, John 189
Saint Bartholomew's Hospital 23
Salem 22
Salonika (now Thessaloniki) 43,44,46
Salisbury Snowfield 129
Saltwater Lagoon 71
Sandison Camera 173
Scopinich, John 37
Scone Creek 226,229
Scone Junction 227
Scotland 2
Scotney, Bonk 229
Scott, Andrew **92**
Scott, Marion 243
Scott's Homestead 134,149
Seaview Hill 31
Seaview Lunatic Asylum 31
Seddon, Richard (Dick) John 17,80
Schürmann, Clamor Wilhelm 18,20,22,23
Sealey Pass 225,227,229
Sealy Range 103,104,142
Seiler Family 212
Sefton, Mt. 185
Sewell Street 15
Shipton, Eric 1
Silberhorn 151
Sir Henty Barkley Hotel 32
Sister of Mercy 53
Snowy Peak 104,207
Somers, Mt. 200
Somme 67
South Australia 18,22
South Island M5
South Westland 41,69,76,77,90,91,97,115,128,193,211
Southern Alps 2,10,144,213,247
Spencer Glacier 117
Spencer, Mt. 217,219,220,222,230
Spencer Valley 4
Speight, Prof. R 83,111,234
Stargazer 190
Stewart,W 83
Stevenson, Nell, 236
Stevenson, R.L. 1,30
Sterling, Prof. E.C. 25
Strachan, Dan, 93
Strachan Pass 93
Strauchon Glacier 132,133
Stocking Glacier 143
Stoddart, Mt.,**204,**205,208
Stoner, Charlie 115,123,**124,**165
Stoner, Harold 115
St. David's Dome 161,164
St. Mary's Clubrooms 53

St. Mildred Peak 129,166
Sullivan, Jack 141, **146,**
Sullivan family 141
Surgeon Superintendent
Sweeney, Robert 36
Swiss Alps 41,83,112,213,214
Swiss Alpine Club 193
Swiss Valleé 4
Switzerland 2,76,211
Sydney 142

Talbot, Mr.222
Tait, Lawson 24
Taramakau River 17,33,231
Tatare Range 116
Tasman, Mt. 26,65,**105**,138,140,185,215,219
Tasman Sea 2,26
Tasman Glacier 2,26,103,130,**131,**132,168
193.194
Teichelmann's Bed and Breakfast 33,246
Teichelmann children: *Frederick, Daniel, Jessie, Christian, Johanna, Charlotte, Margaret,*
Maria, Emmanuel, Theodore, James, Josephine, Johanna Rosina, Alfred 22 (all)
Teichelmann, Charlotte 24,47
Teichelmann, Christian Gottlöb 17, **18,** 19-23
Teichelmann Corner 246
Teichelmann Creek 246
Teichelmann, Ebenezer vii,1-4,13-15, 23-100,**102**-104,106-119,123-147,149-153, 155-157,159-165,169,171-180, 183-191, 193-197,199, 200,202,203,206-217,**217**,219-247, **237,244**
Teichelmann, Friedrich August 17
Teichelmann, Johanna Rosina 17
Teichelmann, Margaret 21,22,24,170
Teichelmann, Mary 3,13,15,**24,** 25- 27, **28,** 29, 96,245
Teichelmann, Mrs. Doctor 29
Teichelmann, Mt., 246
Teichelmann Rock 246
Teichelmann's Track 246
Te Koeti Turanga Runanga, 64
Tekapo 167
Te Koeti, Hera 64
Te Koeti, Butler 47,65
Temple Basin 84
Temple, Philip 98,101
Te Naihi, Ruera **64,**65
Te Wahi Pounamu 247
Thelma Peak 129
Theodule Pass 213
Therma Glacier 103,185
Thiem, Ben 109,110,111
Thomson, Darby 28,193,194,197,211, 212,215,220,**221**
Thornton, C.J, 233
Thorpe, C.E. Rev. 211
Timaru 169
Toll, Dr 25
Tomlinson, Margaret 237
Tony the Greek 115
Tony's Rock 149,150
Torres, Mt. 115,175,243,246
Torrens River 20,22
Tourist and Health Resorts Control Act, 1908
Trustee Savings Bank 3
Turner, B.R., 229
Turner, Sybil 110
Turks 45
Turner, Sybil
Twyneham, R 83
Tyndall, Mt., 104,206,207

USA 80,231

Vanguard 161
Victoria Range 124
Vickers, Mt. 124
Vienna 41
Vollman, Dr.F.W 28,193,195
Von Reiseman, Dagmar 84

Wahapo, Lake 71
Waiatoto River/Valley 63,183,189
Waiho 65,71,74,98,109,125,129,
141,146,159,17,179,180,221
Waiho Gorge 123
Waimakariri 81,233
Waitaha River 71
Walker, J.E., 211
Walter, Mt. 194
Wanganui River/Valley 56,93,97,104,128,198,
202-204,**209**,211,225
Ward, Bob 96
Ward, Jane 96,98
Ward, Tom 96
Waterhole 129,169
Watson, Bruce 90
Weheka 141,146,175
Wellenkuppe, Mt., 213
Wellington 51,54,68
West, Jack, 238
West Coast 2,3,34,40,46,62,81,112,119,
128,145,157,195,214,227
West Coast Acclimatisation Society 78,80,216
West Coast Times 17,32,36,59,78,79,211
Westland 29,41,77,86,106,108,142,229,
232,242
Westland County Council 104
Westland Hospital 3,14,17,25,27,31,40, 235
55,65,115,118,231,245
Westland Hotel 32
Westland Institute 51,59
Westland National Park **85,**90
Westport 235
Whataroa River/Valley
12,71,129,225,226,228
Whiley, Ebenezer 64
Whitcombe Pass 200,202
Whitcombe Valley 123,199,201
White River, 233
Whymper, Edward 213
Whymper, Glacier 11, **12**
Wilberg, Mt., 204
Williams family 175
Williams, Havelock,70,72,73
Wilson, Jim 42,73,151,156,205
Wilson, Ivor 230
Wilson, Mrs. W. 231
Wilson, Ivor 230
Wilson, Mona 230
Wimmera District 21
Wombat Jack 115
Woodham, Arthur 98,116,149-151,195
Woodstock 237
Wright A.F. 78
Wright, Hugh F 211,222
Wyn-Irwin B, 233

Yarrawonga 25
Yorke Peninsula 23

Zeppelin 46
Zermatt 212
Ziman, David 53,**54,**55
Zinal Rothhorn 213
Zurbriggen's Ridge 157
Zurbriggen's Route 151
Zurbriggen's Saddle 124